Abroad

American Expats that Thrive Personally and Professionally Living in Foreign Countries

Abroad: American Expats that Thrive Personally and Professionally Living in Foreign Countries was created by Sara Tyler

Authors: Marco Sison, Nicholas Burns, Gabrielle Smith, Stephanie Wandke, Casey Hearne, Sara Tyler, Hector Grimaldo, and Vincent Reed

Published by Nomad Publishing

Website: https://www.nomadpublishinghouse.com

Copyright © 2024 Nomad Publishing

All rights reserved. No portion of this book may be reproduced in any form without permission from the publisher, except as permitted by U.S. copyright law.

For permissions contact: Sara Tyler by WhatsApp: +52 56 5050 2513

Cover design by 99designs

All photos featured in the book were provided by the individual authors.

1st Edition

INTRODUCTION

Even if you are a frequent international traveler, it's one thing to travel abroad and then return to the comfort of home. It's a completely different level when you sell all your belongings, pack your suitcases, and take a one-way flight out of your home country.

Becoming an expat is a journey that often resembles a rollercoaster. You experience so many different emotions, doubt yourself at times, and take huge personal and professional risks by moving overseas.

This anthology is dedicated to telling the stories of expats and digital nomads who love living abroad, who have created fulfilling personal and professional lives outside of their home country, and most of all, who can't imagine ever going back!

In *Abroad: American Expats that Thrive Personally and Professionally Living in Foreign Countries*, you will read nine uniquely inspiring chapters written by eight expat entrepreneurs currently living outside of their home countries. Authors have committed to sharing their stories, including their ups and downs, in order to encourage others interested in moving abroad to ultimately take the leap.

Contributors work in diverse industries and come from a variety of backgrounds. They have different nationalities, upbringings, educational levels, and life experiences. But, what binds them all together is their common love of adventure and lifelong learning.

In their respective chapters, authors share the personal and professional journeys that helped them build a life abroad.

What exactly do the chapters in this book cover?

Chapter 1: *How to Move Abroad, Retire Early, and Live Your Dream Life* by Marco Sison covers the real numbers and budgets needed to be able to retire as early as in your 30s or 40s in a foreign country as well as the financial benefits expats take advantage of when living abroad.

Chapter 2: *Submarines, Semiconductors, and Singapore: An American Expat Story* by Nicholas Burns details how a foreign U.S. soldier used the skills he gained during his time in the Navy to secure his dream job that brought him around the world, before ending up in Singapore.

Chapter 3: *Boldly Blooming Beyond Borders* by Gabrielle Smith follows a former teacher who lost her job in Mexico due to COVID-19, but managed to turn her own expat experiences into a successful business that helps other foreigners move to Mexico and gives back by employing Mexicans in her local community.

Chapter 4: *Passport to Pivot* by Stephanie Wandke explores the all too common ups and downs of online entrepreneurship while traveling to remote destinations around the world, and how the author found her home and community while growing an in-demand business as an expat living in Merida, Mexico.

Chapter 5: *Afar* by Casey Hearne covers the author's desire to get out of Texas at all costs, and how she became a busy entrepreneur running several local businesses in El Salvador while raising a bilingual child on her own.

Chapter 6: *Live Outside Your Comfort Zone* by Sara Tyler explores how the small town, low-income environment she grew up in limited what she thought was possible in her future, but how traveling and living abroad as a solo female expat allowed her the opportunity to create a life without limits.

Chapter 7: *Operation Overseas* by Stephanie Wandke compares the healthcare system costs and experiences in the U.S. with Cuba and Mexico, as well as her personal experiences having surgery abroad without the support of her family, instead relying on her local expat community to take care of her.

Chapter 8: *Dreamers Are Doers* by Hector Grimaldo details how a Mexican/American English teacher turned ed-techpreneur ended up living in Vietnam, the five-step formula he recommends to make your dreams come true, and the powerful mindset lessons he picked up along the way.

Chapter 9: *Comfortably Uncomfortable* by Vincent Reed explains how a TEFL teacher from a multi-cultural family accepted a challenge from his Dad that led to him teaching and living as an expat in China and Southeast Asia.

And many more obstacles that come up when you decide to make a foreign country your new home.

The stories are collected in a multi-author book format. Multi-author books feature a group of authors and each is responsible for writing one chapter. You can compare them to the *Chicken Soup for the Soul* series that was popular in the 1990s.

That means that you, the reader, receive the benefit of different points of views and experiences surrounding the topic of the book. Each story is unique to the author who wrote it, in writing style, tone, and personality. Some stories emphasize facts and statistics while others focus on individual growth and transformation. They are not meant to flow continuously, but instead, to represent each author individually.

Ready to see if expat life is for you?

Go ahead and start reading.

CHAPTER 1: HOW TO MOVE ABROAD, RETIRE EARLY, AND LIVE YOUR DREAM LIFE

By Marco Sison

While sitting down to write, it is only two days away from Halloween in the United States. While the U.S. is getting ready for a supernatural and spooky holiday, I found some financial retirement data that is freaking scary.

The median retirement savings Americans between forty-five to fifty-four have built up is LESS than $50,000.

Keep in mind that many financial planners recommend you have four times your annual salary saved by forty-five and seven times by fifty-five. With the U.S. median income at roughly $55,000 per year, most Americans in my generation are already waaaaayyy short of their retirement savings.

Even more frightening is the final amount the average

American believes they need to retire comfortably, which rose to $1.8 million last year.

If you are an average fifty-five-year-old Gen X'er, you need to go from $50,000 to $1.8 million in twelve years to comfortably retire in the United States.

Holy Crap!

What's the answer? Make more money?

The average income in the U.S. is already one of the highest in the world.

How about working more?

The USA already ranks third in the country with the LEAST number of vacation days. Some 40% of Americans never take a vacation day in a year. No days off to travel, go to the beach with your kids, or hang out with family.

Is the answer to work longer?

Here is another terrifying fact. You probably can't work longer, even if you want to. Most workers over fifty-five years old are involuntarily forced into retirement due to job loss or health conditions.

Even if you wanted to delay retirement and work into your seventies, you may not have that choice. More than half of us will be forced out of our jobs by circumstances out of our control because of layoffs or health problems.

The situation may seem hopeless, but it's not.

What if I told you I retired fifteen years after I graduated from university?

What if I told you my net worth increased by over 60% even after I stopped working?

Did I inherit that money?

Nope. My family immigrated from a developing country. My mom was a single teenage mother before that was a thing. She literally farmed rice growing up.

"Sure," you think, *"you are probably a ridiculously high-paid software engineer, doctor, lawyer, or Hollywood superstar."*

Nope. My average income in fifteen years of working is roughly $70,000 per year. Decent pay, but not George Clooney good.

Maybe you think I got lucky and was a Silicon Valley start-up genius or lottery winner?

Negative. I wish I could be so fortunate.

My story is far from a fairy tale.

I was behind before I even started working. Because I paid my own way through college, I didn't graduate until I was twenty-seven. To make matters worse, I was crushed with **over $40,000 in student loan debt.**

While working, I went through two major market crashes (the 2000 dot-com bubble and the 2007 great recession) and the 2008 U.S. housing crash. I even nearly went bankrupt after my small business crashed and burned.

Through it all, I kept grinding away at my job. I averaged sixty to seventy hour workweeks, crouched behind a computer screen, and ate meals at my desk. My health was crap, and my relationships suffered. I was caught in the oh-so-familiar corporate American rat race.

Then, after fifteen years of slaving away making my corporate leadership rich (well, richer, let's be honest, they were already millionaires), I was laid off.

What do you do when everything you worked for is taken away?

I had a decision to make. Corporations will not stop squeezing workers for more productivity. They don't care about burnout or exhaustion. They don't want to hear about work/life balance. They just want you to answer emails at nine p.m. and have your personal phone number to call on the weekends.

They quip that the definition of insanity is doing the same thing over and over and expecting different results. If I followed the same path, I would knowingly sacrifice my physical and emotional health.

Or I could try something *different*.

"Traditional life" in the U.S. looks like this:

0 – 18 years old Youth	18 – 67 years old Work	67 – 80 years old Retirement

Eighty years old is the average life expectancy in the U.S. We trade in forty-nine years of work for potentially thirteen years of retirement.

We spend 80% of our adult lives toiling away at a job.

I don't know who came up with that idea, but they're a sadist.

The plus side of being a poor immigrant and having your savings wiped out three times is you learn to live below your means. Even with my middling salary, I squirreled away what I could.

I had a nest egg but nowhere near enough money to retire early in the U.S.

My strategy for early retirement: jump on a plane.

The Fastest Way to Build One Million Dollars in Retirement: Become An Expat

On January 11th, 2020, I officially became a millionaire.

There was no confetti celebration, grand announcement, or cinematic montage.

Just me looking at a cursor on a laptop, my deep breathing the only sound.

$1,000,038 - Seven digits marked the realization of my goal since childhood.

Me. The kid, mocked for wearing his mother's hand-me-down clothes, made it to the two-comma club.

Me. The poor immigrant from a poor country, the first in his family to attend college, is now financially in the **top 6% of the U.S. or the top 0.2% in the world.**

My savings, right before the pandemic hit in 2020, reached $1,000,000.

My net worth when I retired in 2015 was - $600,000. **This means my wealth grew 67% in less than five years.** *Pretty impressive?*

I didn't speculate in crazy stocks, risk my life savings in Bitcoin, and I didn't marry a Nigerian prince.

How did I generate that money doing nothing illegal?

The answer is **geoarbitrage.**

What The Heck Is Geographic Arbitrage?

Arbitrage might sound like a fancy word from the world of economics, but it's a straightforward concept. At its core, arbitrage is all about taking advantage of price differences between different markets.

Think of it like this: *Have you ever driven past your regular grocery store to go to a cheaper one because they had a great deal on the same steaks?* Well, that's a form of arbitrage in action.

Geographic arbitrage (as the kids shorten it these days, geoarbitrage) is arbitrage but with a geographic twist.

Geoarbitrage is about using your location to get more bang for your buck. Just like you'd pay less for those steaks in a cheaper supermarket, you can pay less for rent by choosing an apartment in the suburbs over the posh city center.

Domestic Geoarbitrage

Domestic geoarbitrage offers substantial cost savings without needing long-distance moves. You can reap financial benefits by changing your neighborhood within the same city.

When I took my first job, I had the choice of living in the trendy downtown district or the more affordable suburbs. Choosing a suburb resulted in cheaper apartments, lower transportation expenses because of a shorter commute, and decreased local income and property taxes.

International Geoarbitrage

Now we are cooking with gas. Geoarbitrage gets even more exciting when considering the significant financial opportunities of being an expat. Moving overseas is more complex than moving across town or within the same country, but international geoarbitrage can have a massive economic impact.

For example, I saved about $2,000 to $3,000 yearly when I moved domestically from a city to the suburbs. However, **my annual savings skyrocketed to a whopping $20,000 to $30,000 when I left the U.S. to live abroad.**

Whether you're looking at geoarbitrage options in the U.S. or considering a big international move, the goal remains the same: **make your money work harder for you.**

Just as switching from the city to the suburbs can help you save on taxes, moving from an expensive city like New York to a more budget-friendly state like Alabama can significantly reduce your housing costs.

Now, if you take it up a notch and compare living in a place like San Francisco to more cost-effective countries like the Philippines or Colombia, you could see savings of $2,400+ every month.

Cutting your monthly expenses by over 70% is not just a location change; it's a potential game-changer for your financial future.

The Game-Changing Costs Of Expat Life

Let's compare my spending as an expat with what the Economic Policy Institute (EPI) estimates for an adult living a "modest, but adequate" standard of living in a medium-cost city in the U.S. They estimate a **single adult needs over $48,000 per year for a basic American lifestyle** in a modest studio apartment.

On sheer numbers alone, expat life is better. Over the last two years, **I spent less than $16,000 a year living overseas** in beach towns in Egypt and Vietnam, a vibrant capital city in Argentina, a UNESCO World Heritage town in Mexico, as well as taking long vacations in Malaysia, Montenegro, Morocco, Austria, Portugal, and Peru.

I could go into detail about how my living expenses are not only cheaper abroad but also how my higher living standards allow me luxuries unaffordable in the U.S.

From living in two-bedroom beachfront houses ($650) to hiring a weekly maid service ($10) to frequent ribeye steak dinners ($6) to my hour-long deep tissue massages ($5), my expat lifestyle is far from basic.

But let's focus on the big hitters. You won't save your way to a million-dollar retirement by cutting out $5 massages. You can make the biggest impact by cutting your housing, transportation, taxes, and healthcare costs.

These four expenses make up nearly 80% of the average spending of an American in a mid-cost city in the USA. Focus on making drastic cuts here, and you go a long way to meeting your financial goals.

What does "saving significant money" mean? **How does putting an extra $32,000 a year into your bank sound?**

Monthly Expenses	1 Adult Portland, OR	My Expat Budget	Savings
Housing	$ 1,245	$ 400	$ 845
Local Transportation	$ 828	$ 150	$ 678
Taxes	$ 726	$ 65	$ 661
Health Insurance	$ 370	$ 60	$ 310
Top 4 Living Expenses	**$ 3,169**	**$ 680**	**$ 2,489**
Other Expenses	$ 858	$ 635	$ 223
Total Monthly Expenses	$ 4,027	$ 1,315	$ 2,712
Annual Totals	**$ 48,324**	**$ 15,780**	**$ 32,544**

Housing ($850 savings per month)

When $1,200 just covers renting a modest studio, housing prices in the U.S. have officially hit ridiculous levels. While real estate costs have increased globally, you can still get much more house for your money in other countries.

A prime example is my large two-story, one-bedroom, loft-style house with a swimming pool in Hoi An, Vietnam, just fifteen minutes away from the beach, for $400 monthly.

Transportation ($675 savings per month)

I rarely need a car living abroad. For example, I currently live in Buenos Aires, Argentina, where I use their efficient metro system that comes every five minutes and costs me less than .10 cents per ride.

But it's not just about price.

Living abroad opened my eyes to everything the U.S. does wrong with urban planning. In the U.S., car ownership is a necessity due to a lack of walkability, urban sprawl, and lack of public transit options. Expensive cars and SUVs are cultural norms, and cheap gas only fuels our love for them.

Major cities in Europe don't have strip malls. You can walk to nearly everything.

Need to go to the market? Walk.

How about the doctor? Walk.

Headed to late-night drinks with friends? Maybe take an Uber (only $5 in many countries).

If you don't feel like walking, even in "developing" countries in Europe, like Romania and Bulgaria, public transport is plentiful, efficient, and affordable. Monthly passes for unlimited use of subways, buses, trolleys, and light rail can cost as low as $40.

Healthcare and Insurance ($300+ savings per month)

I pay $60 per month for health insurance outside the U.S. because health insurance prices inside the U.S. are out of control. **Basic U.S. health insurance (bronze level) will set you back more than $11,000 every year**. And if you're aiming for fancier plans like silver or gold, get ready to cough up $14,604 or even $16,032 annually.

It's just getting worse. The premiums Americans pay for healthcare have increased by nearly 50% since 2013. And at an estimated 6% to 8%, they expected 2024 insurance increases to be the most significant one-year increase in decades.

The U.S. is already the most expensive place for health insurance. **Out of the 100 most expensive countries for private health insurance, the United States proudly wears the #1 crown.**

Health insurance in the U.S. is so expensive that 20% of American adults skip necessary medical care due to cost.

But hold on, here's a twist. If you're an American expat in places like Colombia (ranked 19th), Hungary (74th), Romania (76th), or Thailand (78th), you could slash 63% off your medical insurance costs.

Studies estimate that 500,000 Americans file for bankruptcy each year with medical debt. It's a relief to know that I can afford comprehensive healthcare coverage abroad for less than the cost of a Starbucks coffee ($3) in the U.S.

Taxes ($650+ savings per month)

The average American pays over $8,700 in federal, state, and payroll taxes, while **I legally pay almost nothing**. I could go into more detail, but international tax strategies are so unique and precisely tailored to your situation that what works for me may not apply to you.

Understanding foreign earned income exclusion (FEIE), foreign tax credits, and other expat tax benefits is challenging, as these depend on your income level, source of income, residency, and host country.

To find the best way to reduce your taxes, chat with an expat tax professional about establishing tax residency in a non-territorial tax country while leveraging FEIE to potentially cut your income tax to nearly zero.

Cost Cutting On Steroids

Now, let's crunch some numbers and see how international geographic arbitrage can completely change your retirement picture.

First, say hello to Domestic Don.

Don has a university degree, lives and works in an average-cost city in the U.S., and earns the median U.S. income of $55,000 per year before taxes.

Don isn't a big spender. He lives in a basic studio apartment, cooks meals at home, drives thirty minutes each way to work, and enjoys a modest $48,000-a-year lifestyle.

As Don turns the big 4-0 this year, he sets a goal to build up for retirement. His financial planner tells him he needs ten times his salary by the time he hits sixty-seven ($555,000 in retirement savings).

After expenses, Don saves $7,000 annually, which is 13% of his gross income. The average U.S. personal savings rate is only about 4%, so Don is ahead of the game.

He keeps his money in cash (no investments). At the end of twenty-seven years of hard work, he has $162,000 in retirement savings, well short of his $555,000 goal.

Now, say hello to Expat Ellie.

Ellie is the same age, in the same situation, with the same goals, and earns the same salary as Don. But she knows that starting to save for retirement at forty is late.

To speed up her retirement savings, she leverages a geoarbitrage strategy by finding a remote job where she can live as an expat in a low-cost country like Vietnam.

Remember the game-changing costs of expat life I mentioned earlier?

Monthly Expenses	Expat Ellie	Savings As An Expat Vs. Living In The USA
Housing	$ 400	$ 845
Local Transportation	$ 150	$ 678

Taxes	$ 65	$ 661
Health Insurance	$ 60	$ 310
Top 4 Living Expenses	**$ 680**	**$ 2,489**
Other Expenses	$ 635	$ 223
Total Monthly Expenses	$ 1,315	$ 2,712
Annual Totals	**$ 15,780**	**$ 32,544**

Ellie only spends $16,000 living a fab expat life overseas, complete with massages, manicures, and maid service. Even while enjoying a higher standard of living, she still saves $32,000 a year, over four times more than Domestic Don in his basic studio apartment in the U.S.

At the end of twenty-seven years, she has put away $864,000 cash in her bank account, hitting 156% of her $555,000 retirement goal.

$32,000 per year saved x twenty-seven years = $864,000 Total Savings for Retirement

It sounds like Ellie is doing very well. *She is winning the expat game of life, right?*

What if I told you that Ellie should be a multi-millionaire expat instead?

Making Your Money Work Harder

Trimming your expenses and saving money is just the beginning. If you stick to simply saving like Ellie, your money is lazy. Uninvested cash is like a couch potato on a Netflix binge - it gets comfortable but doesn't put in any effort to improve itself.

To maximize the advantages of geographic arbitrage, let's make our money work for us by investing.

The power of investing lies in the concept of compound interest (sometimes called compound growth), a financial idea Albert Einstein dubbed the "8th wonder of the world."

Your initial savings earn money, and that extra money makes even more. The more you invest, the harder your money works for you and the faster your wealth compounds. It's like a money snowball that grows faster the more you add to it.

Let's see how compounding works with some numbers.

	Year 1	Year 2	Year 3	...	Year 20
Beginning Investment	$ 100	$ 110	$ 121	...	$ 612
10% Growth Rate	$ 10	$ 11	$ 12	...	$ 61
Total Balance	$ 110	$ 121	$ 133	...	$ 673

This table shows the compound growth of $100 invested over twenty years with a 10% annual growth rate.

- In Year 1, you make 10% on the initial $100, which is $10. The following year, you get your first taste of compounding.
- In Year 2, you make 10% on the initial $100 + the $10 you made in Year 1. Instead of $10, you make $11.
- In Year 3, the snowball grows as your money compounds again. You make 10% on the $100 + the $10 from Year 1 and the $11 in Year 2. Your money makes $12.10 in Year 3. Let's fast forward 20 years and see what your money snowball looks like.
- By Year 20, your initial $100 investment is earning over $61. Your money is working overtime.

Without you investing any more money after the first $100 and without you working, your money was working for you. Your initial $100 investment generates over $60 a year and is now worth $673. And the biggest bonus is you didn't have to do anything but wait.

That is the magic of **compound growth.** The more you have

invested, the more you earn each year.

Turning Dollars Into Millions: Riding the Geoarbitrage Wave

Now, let's bring this "making your money work harder" theory to life with real numbers and see how geoarbitrage + investing can seriously turbocharge your retirement investments over twenty-seven years.

	Year 5	Year 10	Year 20	Year 27
Geoarbitrage Savings - Cash In Bank	$ 160,000	$ 320,000	$ 640,000	$ 864,000
Geoarbitrage + Compound Growth @ 7%	$ 190,914	$ 461,559	$ 1,389,138	$ 2,552,284
% Turbocharged	19%	44%	117%	195%

The top row shows Ellie's cash savings growing without investing. She saves $32,000 annually; after twenty-seven years, she is sitting on $864,000 cash.

Now look at the second row. **Let's see what happens when you combine the savings of geographic arbitrage with compound growth investing.**

But instead of just saving, Ellie invests in a total market ETF (exchange trade fund) or any other lower-risk investment that grows 7% per year. To take advantage of compound growth, she reinvests dividends and keeps all her savings in ETFs for twenty-seven years.

Ellie rocketed her retirement savings to over $2.5 MILLION! She has nearly 200% more cash to spend in retirement thanks to her compound growth investment strategy.

She can celebrate with several daiquiris and dinners by the beach with that kind of savings.

Expat Life and Geographic Arbitrage
Drives Financial Freedom

Does Ellie's story sound too good to be true? It isn't. I am living it. Becoming an expat and leveraging the potential of geographic arbitrage was my ticket to financial freedom.

I went from being a poor immigrant to retiring early at forty-one to explore the world. While I may have yet to hit Ellie's $2.5 million, I'm on the right path.

However, it's about more than just money. I could have pursued a corporate job, kept grinding away, and followed the conventional route to a more "traditional life."

I watched many of my peers tread that very path, weighed down by student loans, crushed beneath the burden of car payments and mortgages. They were caught in the corporate rat race, with an uncertain retirement date looming somewhere in their sixties or seventies.

So, the real question is: *Do you want to keep working fifty, sixty, or even seventy hours a week, being a cog in someone else's wheel, all while hoping for a distant retirement at sixty-seven?* I didn't, and I still don't. **I crave a life filled with experiences, not just endless work.**

Being an expat grants me a higher quality of life at a fraction of the cost, allows for personal growth, and immerses me in diverse cultures. Geoarbitrage provides me the financial independence to prioritize relationships, family, and experiences over work.

That is the life-changing power of living abroad, geographic arbitrage, and compound growth.

AUTHOR MARCO SISON

Marco entered the corporate rat race at some of the world's largest companies after graduating from a top 10 business school. After fifteen years in finance making other people rich, he was downsized and laid off. Rather than letting job loss define him, he wrenched back the reins of his financial future and retired overseas at forty-one.

As a retirement coach with Nomadic FIRE, Marco's expertise in personal finance and expat life abroad led to features in USA Today, U.S. News and World Reports, MSN Money, Yahoo Finance, HuffPost, and numerous other international media, including an iTunes documentary on financial independence.

But success didn't come easy. After a humble beginning as a poor immigrant from a developing country, he faced homelessness, job loss, two stock market crashes, and a failed small business. He wiped his life savings out— twice.

Despite these setbacks and starting his adult life with $40,000 in student loan debt, Marco's uncommon approach of combining the benefits of living abroad with modern investment strategies rebuilt his life and finances, leading to early retirement in his forties.

But Marco doesn't believe retiring means settling down. Retirement isn't the finish line but the start of a new adventure.

"Retirement means you're just getting started. Now, the world is your playground."

Marco's mission to reinvent retirement has led him to over fifty countries, spanning nearly every continent. By utilizing geographic arbitrage, he enjoys a higher quality of life as an expat at a significantly lower cost of living than in the United States.

He shares his practical financial independence strategies and insights as an author and Retirement Coach on Nomadic FIRE. Through his platform, Marco breaks down complex financial concepts into an understandable financial freedom roadmap for a community of 500,000+ expats looking for a better life beyond the traditional U.S. corporate grind.

Are you burned out from the 9-to-5 struggle and looking for a better alternative abroad?

Want to stop just scraping by in the U.S. and build a thriving life overseas?

Want to know what expat life is really like?

Reach out to Marco at:

https://marcosison.com/abroad

Given his past struggles and humble beginnings, Marco believes that his example stands as a testament that an expat life of financial independence and overseas adventure is within reach of everyone with the right mindset and system.

CHAPTER 2: SUBMARINES, SEMICONDUCTORS, AND SINGAPORE: AN AMERICAN EXPAT'S STORY

By Nicholas Burns

Growing up in Connecticut

Growing up in Connecticut, I thought I would live a fairly typical life. Go to school, get a job, travel domestically once or twice a year on vacations, and maybe travel overseas a handful of times in my life. From sixteen to eighteen years old, I did summer internships at Pratt & Whitney and Sikorsky Aircraft, and I imagined I would just grow up to work at a place like that.

Becoming a Submariner

I enlisted in the U.S. Navy in 2011 as a nuclear electronics technician. I spent six years in the Navy, and I got to live in South Carolina, New York, and Hawaii as a result. I had a choice to volunteer for submarines or stay on the surface of the water on an aircraft carrier. My Dad was a submariner, so that was a pretty big influence on my decision. Not only was he a submariner, but he also worked on the nuclear part of submarines. So, that was part of my decision to volunteer for submarine service.

Another reason is that it seemed like a bigger challenge. Compared to an aircraft carrier where you have internet, Starbucks, and even occasional *Amazon* deliveries, being on a submarine was going to be much more challenging, and I was up for it. Living with no fresh air, no windows, and locked in a steel tube underwater for months on end - this is what I wanted to do.

I was sent to the USS Bremerton based in Pearl Harbor, Hawaii. I couldn't wait to go to Hawaii, and the islands exceeded my expectations. Although around half of my time there was spent underwater, the half of it spent on land was an amazing experience. I made great friends with people on my submarine as well as civilians out in town.

We would maximize the use of our off-the-submarine time by going to concerts, camping, hiking, hosting house parties, and going on party boats. While on the submarine, it was nearly always a test of one's ability to withstand horrible conditions. Smelly people, frequently interrupted sleep, eighteen-hour days instead of twenty-four-hour days, and "hot racking."

Hot racking is when three men share two beds. One of the three will always be awake and doing their primary job, leaving two beds open for sleep theoretically. At the end of the work shift, someone would wake up and start doing their primary job. By the time you go back to the bed, it could still be hot from the last person's body. Hence, the term "hot racking" was born.

To make it worse, at times the showers and laundry were paused for an extended period of time to conserve water. Making water is noisy, so we would need to stop showering and washing clothes to stay as quiet as possible. This plus "hot racking" made for a truly nightmarish life at times.

On the submarine, I was deployed to the Western Pacific during 2015 and 2016 where we had port calls in Okinawa, Sasebo, South Korea, Guam, and Singapore. Singapore stood out as an amazing country due to the diversity, food, safety, and interesting people doing interesting jobs. I was amazed at this tiny city-state enclave in Southeast Asia with a higher per capita GDP than the U.S., a comfortable standard of living, and openness to foreigners. I fantasized about what it would be like to live in such a cool place.

I thought to myself, *"What would it be like to live in a place where public transit is ubiquitous, clean, safe, and always on time?"* or, *"What would it be like to live in a place where you can feel safe if you leave your phone and laptop out in the cafe when you go to the toilet?"*

Perhaps most enticingly, *"What would it be like to live in a place where you could travel to Bali, Vietnam, Thailand, or countless other places in a cheap, quick, weekend trip for less than the price of a weekend going out to nightclubs?"*

Journey to Move Abroad

Getting Out of the Navy: I was always dead set on not re-enlisting. Instead, I would give the U.S. Navy six years of my life in return for a few good experiences, mostly bad experiences, and a lot of good technical training that I can use in the civilian world.

For nuclear-trained personnel especially, the U.S. Navy gives big bonuses to encourage people to re-enlist. At the time, you could get up to a six-figure bonus for a two-year extension of your contract. I tried to tell as many people as possible to not sign the dotted line. Instead, become a civilian and enjoy a better life.

From my observations, in general, those who stay in the Navy are afraid to take the jump because the U.S. Navy gives you a relatively comfortable life. It is extremely difficult to get fired, so if you are a poor performer, you can rise through the ranks just by continuing to re-enlist. There are some great leaders in the Navy, but there are also many who get promoted only because they keep re-enlisting. Then, these bad leaders lower the morale of their sailors, and the cycle continues. Those bad leaders try to get the younger sailors to re-enlist since it makes them look better.

They will say things like, *"There aren't any jobs out there,"* or *"This person left the Navy and the best job he could find was handing out basketballs at the YMCA."*

The people I looked up to the most were those who got out of the Navy to do something else. To those people who joined the Navy so they could see other parts of the world, I wanted to show them that you can get paid to take an airplane to Singapore as opposed to a submarine. By the way, taking a flight to Singapore is much better than taking a submarine.

Beach Bum: After my six years in the Navy, my original plan was to take some time off to relax and go to the beach in Hawaii every day. I used to go camping on the beach whenever I had the chance, and I envied those civilians who got to do that all of the time. I wanted to be a beach bum for a while in Hawaii to decompress from my time in the submarine. I grew sick of it after around a month and decided to start interviewing for jobs.

Nuclear-trained people in the Navy are pretty heavily sought after in the civilian world, so I didn't have much trouble setting up interviews. Ultimately, I moved to Los Angeles briefly while interviewing at SpaceX and Tesla. Tesla gave me a job offer first, and I moved to San Francisco to work for them in 2017.

San Francisco: I loved living in San Francisco, but I didn't love the commute across the Bay to work at the Tesla Factory. I had some gripes and complaints about working at Tesla – relatively low pay for the Bay Area, unsafe working conditions, and pretty easy problems to solve – to name a few. Mostly, the work was too boring for me.

Luckily, I had some great coworkers who taught me a lot about working in the civilian world, and this was a great transition job for me out of the military. I quit after five months and took a high-travel job as a technical support engineer at KLA-Tencor (now called KLA Corporation). This was my first exposure to the semiconductor industry.

I was traveling all the time for work, flying across the globe (South Korea, Japan, Singapore, Israel, Germany, and Ireland) to fix machines that were extremely complex. Most of the time, the travel was under an emergency situation and there was not much notice. So, I frequently had to fly across the world in only a day or so after being told I was needed. I liked the excitement and the challenge.

These semiconductor machines are more complex to maintain than nuclear reactors. That scratched the itch I had to solve challenging problems at work. At Tesla, the equipment did have problems from time to time, but the solution was a simple reset normally. If it couldn't be fixed by a simple reset or a few actions in a technical manual, we called the vendor for help. Working at the cutting edge of the semiconductor field is great because you work in teams with some of the smartest people in the industry. The most job satisfaction I get is when the team solves a very challenging problem that takes a lot of collaboration to get through.

For those people considering a career change or looking for an exciting, fulfilling job, the United States needs a lot of semiconductor workers as the U.S. attempts to increase its semiconductor manufacturing posture. The United States government and foreign semiconductor companies are investing in facilities in the United States, so there are many job openings that need to be filled in this critical industry. It is a good industry for someone with a technical background and excellent troubleshooting skills.

My exposure to Singapore also increased a lot in my role at

KLA. Most of the training I did at work was in Singapore, so I spent many months there, living a pretty nice life in a nice hotel for months on end. During this time, I met even more people who lived and worked there–locals as well as expatriates. Most of the expatriates I met loved living in Singapore, and I made it my mission to move there one day.

After spending so much time abroad, I started to feel happier when I was overseas working compared to when I was working in the U.S. It was getting to be embarrassing to be an American overseas when I was working and there was another school shooting or a politician said something crazy on *Twitter*. It was always hard to explain these American problems to people overseas, but then eventually it became hard for me to reconcile it for myself too.

How can I pay so much tax living in San Francisco when I see so many problems outside of my home?

I felt more and more connected to Asia as opposed to California or the U.S.

Singapore

I kept floating the idea with my boss of moving to Singapore, and finally, it looked like it might be possible. While I could have applied for jobs directly in Singapore, the country is fairly strict with working visas. While not impossible, it is much easier to transfer there for your work. Whenever I went to Singapore, I told my colleagues there that I was trying to move there, and it seemed like a half-joke at the time because it seemed so impossible and far-fetched to me.

Towards the end of 2019, it started to look like we could open another position for our team in Singapore. Then, I had to apply although it was a horizontal transfer. It was the exact same job I was doing but based in Singapore instead of Silicon Valley. In January of 2020, I donated or sold all of my belongings that couldn't fit in two suitcases and a backpack, then I took the long-awaited one-way flight to Singapore. I couldn't wait to hear the chopping sounds from chicken rice stalls, smell the spices from outstanding Indian restaurants, and taste what I would argue is the best collection of food in the world.

As soon as I landed in Singapore, I needed to settle in as quickly as possible to go to Israel for a work assignment. As soon as I could, I found an apartment to rent, opened a bank account, and finished all of our onboarding paperwork at work. Then, I left for Israel soon after I arrived in Singapore. At that time, COVID-19 was starting to spread across the globe. While in Israel, they banned travelers from Singapore and other countries. Then, more and more countries announced closures, so I returned to Singapore to ensure I wouldn't be stranded overseas.

My company's ability to fly engineers across the world to fix things abruptly ended. Our customers kept using the tools, and the machines still needed to be repaired. My company pivoted away from "fly and fix" to using augmented reality in order to "see what I see" models of troubleshooting.

If there was a problem with a machine in France, in the past, I would just fly to France to fix it. During COVID-19 lockdowns, this was not possible. Instead, we used augmented reality solutions so I could sit in my home office in Singapore and direct the repair in France. An engineer in France would wear AR glasses so I could see what he was seeing. Then, I could tell him to adjust this, turn this knob, replace this, or do any number of things that were required to fix the tool. This greatly accelerates the repair time when compared to the alternative of waiting for borders to open.

After stopping my high business travel, I fell further in love with Singapore and was happy to settle down a bit and stop traveling as much. Luckily, as the world started to reopen for travel, I was promoted to now manage a team of engineers. This meant less business travel. It was bittersweet losing my highest levels of airline and hotel loyalty statuses, but now I don't miss all the time spent to reach those levels. Now, when I travel, it is to go on holiday or visit family and friends.

Why Singapore?

For a Westerner, Singapore is Asia in easy mode. English is spoken by almost everyone, so there is rarely a language barrier unless you go to some Chinese restaurants. I have studied Chinese for a couple of years now, but it isn't necessary to live here. I study it because it is easy to practice every day. A good number of people you interact with in the world here speak Mandarin in addition to English (and other languages too). I take in-person Chinese lessons to hold me accountable for keeping up with vocabulary and grammar. I've also scored highly on the first two levels of Chinese competency exams (HSK-1 and HSK-2), administered by Hanban, which is a part of the Ministry of Education of the People's Republic of China.

Singapore is wildly safe compared to where I used to live (SoMa and the Tenderloin in San Francisco). I never feel unsafe walking around any part of Singapore, regardless of the time of day. If I go to a bus stop at night in Singapore, I know I will never encounter someone high on drugs, begging for money, or acting threateningly.

Contrast this with walking around at night in San Francisco, and it seems like a different world. If I took the train back from Oakland to downtown San Francisco at night, or if I walked home from a concert in San Francisco, it felt very unsafe. People would get mugged, you would see open-air drug use and deals, and the overall threat level meant you never truly felt safe walking around. When I go back to any major U.S. city, I am reminded of how safe we live in Singapore.

U.S. expatriates also enjoy a much lower effective U.S. tax rate if they live abroad – as long as they spend less than thirty-five days in the United States in any given year. Contrasting with the U.S., the Singapore tax system is very simple too!

During tax season, I get an SMS message from the government saying that my taxes are done. They say to log in and check everything, and if I agree, no action is required. The due taxes are deducted from my next year's paychecks to cover the previous year. This puts the U.S. tax system to shame, especially if you are doing U.S. taxes as an expat.

U.S. expats face the unpleasant reality of citizenship-based taxation. Even if I were to never return to the U.S. for the rest of my life, I would still need to pay taxes there every year. That is, unless I renounce my citizenship. That being said, the effective tax rate is much lower than that of someone living in the U.S., and especially California.

My dream one day is to become a Singapore citizen so I can renounce my U.S. citizenship. This way, I can finally be totally free from the U.S. tax system. As a non-U.S. citizen, I can also have the freedom to be in the United States for more than thirty-five days a year without suffering a gigantic tax burden.

Culture Shock

I had the benefit of having spent a decent amount of time "living" in Singapore before moving, so I had a good idea of what to expect. To most people in the world, the price of rent would be considered very high. To someone moving from San Francisco, the rent is normal. People say that the work/hustle culture in Singapore is toxic, but it is a more relaxed working environment than San Francisco and Silicon Valley. As someone who had driven a car since I was sixteen years old, I wasn't sure how I would enjoy not having a car.

At the time of writing, it costs over $100,000 USD for the right to own a car for ten years in Singapore. Then, you have to pay for a more expensive car on top of that. So, a basic Toyota Camry Hybrid costs $183,000 USD in Singapore as opposed to less than $29,000 USD for the same car in the U.S. Luckily, the train system

(MRT) and buses cover the whole city and that is what most Singaporeans use to get around.

Singapore's laws are also quite different than in the U.S. There is a mandatory death penalty by hanging for illegal drugs. The government can force you to correct something you said online if they consider it to be false. Caning is used as corporal punishment for some crimes, including overstaying your visa by ninety days, vandalism, and other more serious crimes. There is also no freedom of speech or freedom of assembly like there is in the United States. You cannot protest something or hold up a sign in public without being shut down by the police. This is a different way of running society, and many of the people here think it is better and it will prevent some of the negative parts of living in a totally free, Western society.

Overall, I think Singapore's system of government is the best in the world, and I think it is a better place to live than the United States.

Most Americans live within eighteen miles of their Mom. If you ask my Mom, I'm sure she would prefer that I live eighteen miles away from her as opposed to my current distance of over 9,400 miles, but I didn't want to become one of those American statistics.

Only one-third of Americans have a valid U.S. passport. Living as an expat in Southeast Asia, I get to enjoy cheap travel to nearby countries that wouldn't otherwise be possible. Living as an expat has exposed me to different cultures, different ways of life, and different ways of thinking. I am incredibly lucky to have had the opportunity to live abroad.

Lessons Learned

I've tried to be an ambassador for people to take the chance. Get out of the military (especially the Navy) and try your luck as a civilian. Turn down that $100,000 bonus to get back two years of your life from the military. Switch industries to something totally different than your current job. Take that overseas assignment at work. Start that business. Take the chance no matter what it is.

AUTHOR
NICHOLAS BURNS

Nicholas Burns is an American living abroad since January 2020. He grew up in Connecticut, but has also lived in Philadelphia, South Carolina, New York, Hawaii, and San Francisco.

He was previously a U.S. Navy submariner as a nuclear electronics technician onboard the USS Bremerton based in Pearl Harbor, Hawaii. He has worked in the United States, South Korea, Japan, Germany, Israel, Ireland, and Singapore.

He lives in Singapore with his wife Jessica and their dog named Kahloo. At work, he currently manages a team of engineers in the semiconductor industry for KLA Corporation covering Asia and Europe.

In his free time, he enjoys playing chess online, studying Chinese, and traveling around Southeast Asia. Aside from his family and friends, the biggest thing he misses about the United States is the Mexican food, especially having lived in San Francisco.

Connect with Nicholas here:

https://www.linkedin.com/in/nicholas-burns-eng

CHAPTER 3: BOLDLY BLOOMING BEYOND BORDERS

By Gabrielle Smith

January 20th, 2000

Twenty-five strangers and I boarded an airplane from Phoenix to Mexico City to embark on a three-and-a-half-month Spanish immersion program in Cuernavaca, Mexico. Having been surrounded by Mexican culture and the Spanish language my entire life, I was excited, nervous, and determined to learn Spanish. What I didn't realize was that this short time in Mexico would turn into a lifelong love affair.

Arriving in Mexico, we were ushered through immigration, bright-eyed and buzzing with excitement and nerves. Loaded onto the bus south to Cuernavaca, I had no idea what to expect. I'd spent weeks researching and reading tour guides (long before the days of *Google* and *Pinterest*) and flipping through the pages of the school's catalog. I couldn't wait for the adventure to begin.

Arriving at the school, we were met by our host family, a lovely set of parents and three children around our age who would be key in the formation of my "Mexican" identity, taking me under their wings as if I had always been a part of the family and teaching me all the ways of Mexican language and culture. The program ended, but my relationship with my host family did not. I returned as often as I could, during school vacations for weeks and months on end. As life continued to move along, my trips to Mexico became fewer and further between, but in the back of my head, I never stopped dreaming about returning to live here again someday.

Seventeen years later, I began seriously researching a move abroad, with Mexico being at the top of my list of course. I joined several international teaching agencies, and got a phone call from an agency, Teacher's Latin America, who wanted to place me with a school in Mexico City. I went through the interview process and was offered the position, but for some reason, the offer didn't end up panning out. I decided to take a trip to both Houston and Mexico City to attend their job fairs where I was offered positions in both Queretaro and Monterrey. But, my heart was set on Mexico City.

I put the idea to rest as I was working on not only the last bit of my doctoral dissertation but also my school principal certification and teaching full-time. I decided that I would start to research it again more seriously once the time was right. In June of 2019, I finished my Ph.D. and was looking for jobs in school leadership. Considering moving to various parts of the U.S. and the world for whatever was the best fit for me. I'd kind of let the Mexico City dream fade away, until one day on November 9th, 2019, out of the blue, I received an incoming phone call from a Mexico City phone number. Driving to the airport for my grandpa's 90th birthday party, I just knew I had to answer it.

"Gabriela? Soy Pola. ¿Cómo andas? ¿Cómo has estado? No se si recuerdas de mi, pero estamos buscando una coordinadora de inglés para la primaria y pensamos en ti. ¿Te interesa?"

And there it was, the moment I'd stopped thinking about it, the moment I'd completely let any planning or effort out the window, the opportunity to return to Mexico, specifically Mexico City, fell in my lap.

Within nine weeks (with a previously planned two-week trip to Europe for the Christmas markets thrown in there), I packed up everything I owned into two storage units (with no shortage of blood, sweat, tears, curse words, and the help of my mom and uncle) with the intentions of coming home at spring break to deal with it, threw some necessities in a couple of moving boxes to take with me, got my dog prepped for airline travel, and was ready for my new adventure in Mexico City. Although slightly disappointed that my apartment was going to be located in Mexico State, bordering Mexico City, I was still excited for this new adventure to start. It was my first leadership position in a school, I was living in my soul country, and getting the opportunity to put international experience on my resume.

Win. Win. Win.

January 2nd, 2020

Almost twenty years to the day that I had first landed in Mexico City to study abroad, I boarded a flight from Arizona to Mexico City again, this time with no expiration date. My dog, three cardboard moving boxes, and a suitcase were all I had brought for my new adventure. I'd be back soon to take care of all the loose ends (*and oh let me tell you, there were many*).

I was picked up at the airport by the school's driver who took me to my new apartment, a ninth-floor unit with floor-to-ceiling windows in a high rise with heavy security. I was met by the director and recruiter for H.R. who warmly welcomed me with basics for the apartment and a sweet welcome basket of Mexican goodies.

Four days later, I was getting picked up to start my first day at my very new job: new country, private school, new grade level, new position, new team. From the moment I set foot on campus I was impressed, but shocked. Having come from the U.S. where I had worked mainly in underserved schools with youth who had spent significant time in the juvenile justice system, I was used to security, mainly in the form of metal detectors and metal detector wands. Here we had to check in and out at multiple security gates and check in and out any personal items we brought into school (in my case a portable space heater).

My team quickly welcomed me with open arms, showing me the ropes as I tried to adapt to my new role and new environment halfway through the school year. It was more challenging than I ever imagined it would be. Although I spoke fluent Spanish, had attended school myself in Mexico (albeit, a language immersion program at a university), and had years of educational experience below the belt, this was a whole new ballgame.

I left many days frustrated trying to figure out how to best fill my role, while also adapting to everything around me. One of the most frustrating things for me was the isolation I felt living so far away from the city in an area that really required a car. I would do my best to get into the city as much as possible on the weekends, but weeknights were 100% out of the question due to traffic.

I threw myself into working, learning how to be a better leader, English instruction pedagogy, and just anything related to my job in general. I was also struggling with the altitude, something people don't think about much when they think of Mexico, and was battling colds and sinus issues and sheer exhaustion on the daily. A few weeks into work, I was already having to call in sick.

After about six weeks, I felt like everything was starting to fall into place. My residency card had finally been printed, my Mexican bank account opened, and I'd even started to make some friends, enrolled in French classes, and was exploring the city on the weekends. I'd also picked up an online job as a university teaching assistant in the U.S. for a business course to help supplement my *peso* income.

In the background of all of this however, was the world news and chatter about a new "virus" taking the countries by storm. Here in Mexico, however, there had been no such attack and thus things moved along slowly, but you could see the fear and the energy surrounding it.

Repeatedly my boss would say in meetings, "*We're going to have to close, there's no doubt we'll close like they did last time.*" She was speaking in reference to the swine flu or another worldwide virus.

As the weeks went on and the world news became more grave, we started to have contingency plans, what-if plans, and staff meetings ensuring the staff that someone was checking the public health information regularly and that "to date" no reported cases of this "covid virus" had been documented in Mexico.

Until there was.

Ten weeks after stepping foot onto my new campus, all staff was sent home for a "long weekend." A long weekend that turned into months, that turned into a year of relearning everything we all knew about education. Instead of in-person classes, we had hours after hours of Zoom meetings. Teachers had to rapidly learn how to use online resources to teach their students. Elementary school students were thrown into the world of computer usage at a level never presented to them before. That year and a half was, well, let's call it unique.

Compounded with the online academic existence, living alone in what I called my Rapunzel tower, life got really challenging. I'd moved to Mexico with a budget based on the very consistent U.S. to Mexican-peso exchange rate, which took a complete nosedive once the pandemic hit.

My weekends socializing in the city turned into virtual game nights. My trip back to the U.S. at spring break to tie up loose ends, was canceled. I was holding on by a thread, living alone in this foreign yet not really, but still yes, foreign, country during a worldwide pandemic, with nothing but my dog and a virtual community to rely on, in addition to drowning financially.

My salary crashed due to the peso nosedive. My tenant in my rental property in the U.S. moved out, so for the first time in fifteen years my unit was vacant, and I was trying to make everything work while also making twenty percent less of my income. I wanted to throw in the towel, but even that wasn't an option.

I had moved to Mexico to live my dream and dammit I was going to make it work. Not to mention the logistics of trying to go back would have been a nightmare. I'd be homeless, jobless, and moneyless, with a dog, a suitcase, and three moving boxes. Slowly I tried to make the best of it, facetime with family, virtual game nights, virtual church, virtual French classes, and I picked up another side job that helped the financial hemorrhaging. Slowly I began to adjust to this *"encerrada"* lifestyle, but REALLY wanted to be in the city.

If I wasn't going to be going to school daily, what was the point of living in a Rapunzel tower in the middle of nowhere?

Begging H.R. for weeks, things finally began to take a turn, since we were still working virtually, and it appeared we would be for the unforeseen future. I was allowed to move apartments. I ran from my high-security Rapunzel tower towards a family-owned three-unit building steps from the largest park in all of Latin America. I was finally able to walk my dog, and buy coffee in a coffee shop (albeit from a distance, wearing a mask), but I developed human connections.

Finally!

My Mexican life that I had dreamed of was starting to develop, slowly, cautiously, but surely. I walked in the park, I started a volunteer dog shelter walking group that became a regular

Saturday afternoon "pandemic friendly" activity where I grew a core group of friends from around the world, and then finally, eleven and a half months after arriving in Mexico, I boarded a plane home to Arizona to "tie up loose ends."

What was supposed to be a ten-day trip home, turned into five weeks. With no return to campus in sight, I chose to stay back in Phoenix and spend more time with my family. Working three jobs from my computer in my parents' living room, I still never doubted I had made the right decision, yet, I was finding it hard to bring myself to go back to Mexico, and would call regularly to change my flight back later and later and later.

I finally returned in late January, still working online. I'd gotten used to it at this point, and the thought of actually going back to campus, a campus I didn't really even know, was hard to imagine. Eventually, it looked as if the world sloooowwwlllly might start opening up. A glimmer of someone working from campus, a meeting discussing having students at school. Eventually, in April we returned to school on a very alternative schedule, being able to keep students separated while also managing the staff's varying schedules.

One morning in mid-June, I was sitting in the office with a couple of other coordinators and the sub-director. Always one to have a good "gut feeling" intuition, I could tell something was up.

A few minutes later, I was called to the director's office, where my director took my hands and looked at me with tears in her eyes and said, "*We are terminating your contract effective at the end of the school year.*" This was in two weeks.

She explained that they absolutely adored me, and if it weren't for the pandemic, and the economic situation the school was facing, they would one hundred percent keep me on board, but it was just not viable. And I totally understood.

In all honesty, I was surprised it had taken that long to let me go, and I was a little relieved. As much as I had enjoyed my time there, the position wasn't the best fit for me, nor was I for the position (at least from what I could tell since I never actually got the chance to DO my job). Even my assistant director pulled me aside later and sat me down to be sure that I understood that I was overqualified for the position and that she hoped that a year from now, I would be doing something MUCH bigger and a better fit for me and that we'd go to dinner at a fancy restaurant that I would pay for of course because I had made it to that bigger and better place.

That relief, however, was overshadowed by the panic that quickly set in. I was sent to H.R. to discuss the terms, as part of my benefits package as a foreign hire included my apartment. The school paid for it and the lease was in their name. The thought of having to leave this apartment that I loved so much, with neighbors who had become friends, with a dog sitter around the corner, was not an option.

It. JUST. WASN'T.

Yet my lease was up at the end of July.

How on earth would I get the landlord to rent to me again, or if not that landlord, another one, with no proof of income and no cosigner?

For a couple of days, I sat around and sobbed frantically calling the property manager, discussing options, her calling the landlord, and me waiting for answers, while also trying to figure out what on earth I was going to do to sustain myself financially. I'd finally hit a stride, started to catch up with the three jobs I was working, gotten a tenant in my rental property in the States, the peso was recovering, I'd sold off stuff at Christmas and paid off a little debt, but I still wasn't in no position to not be working full-time.

Sticking my 40-something-year-old tail between my legs, I called my father. The landlord had agreed to renew my lease with the terms that I pay three months' rent upfront plus one month's deposit. At this point, I would have given her an ovary if she'd asked for it. But at the moment, I didn't have that kind of money. My dad generously offered to pay the upfront rent while I looked for a job and waited for my severance from the school.

With Maslow's first level of basic needs covered, it was time to decide what to do about income. I quickly got another job working in college consulting, but the position I had been recruited for and interviewed for, was filled by someone else, and I was given a different position not at all aligned with my skills and knowledge. However, desperate for income and empty promises of quickly being promoted, I took the position as the salary was great for Mexican terms, and I still had my other jobs.

I proceeded to simultaneously search for other employment though, deciding that at this point, my best bet would have to be an online job in the U.S. With so many expenses in dollars, I couldn't take the risk of another *peso* crash, and not knowing when or what might collapse underneath me again financially. As I searched and searched for more jobs, my agent from the education recruitment agency reached out to me.

Over the course of the pandemic, we had become good friends, forming a WhatsApp "quaranteam" and having socially distanced gatherings to keep our sanity. He had begun puttering around in the world of visas and immigration, as a school recruiter, he was well-versed in the topic and found a stream of income for himself after answering questions from folks on *Facebook* groups regarding the residency process. He brought me on to help him.

For every person he obtained via a *Facebook* post where I recommended him, he would give me a commission. After just a short month and a half of this, his client load had taken off so well that he offered to teach me how to do them myself, and I began taking on my own clients. We became quite the pair, hosting information sessions at coffee shops, taking social media by storm answering questions, and obtaining more clients. I was learning loads of information, while also finally able to stop the financial hemorrhaging that had begun during the pandemic.

We started splitting the cases, him taking the hard-to-solve ones, and me the standard ones. We expanded our knowledge exponentially, learning everything we could about the world of Mexican immigration law, even enrolling in an online Mexican immigration law certification program. Then one day, everything really changed for me. While hosting an informational session at a Condesa coffee shop, a potential client, who also happened to be a YouTuber, asked if I would be willing to do a *YouTube* video about the immigration process. Happily, I agreed.

It was getting close to Christmas and immigration closing for the year, but we agreed on an early December interview. Not really into *YouTube* myself, I had no clue what to expect. In my mind, this wasn't a business, but more of just a side hustle to help people make the residency process easier while also being able to make more money than my English teaching jobs were paying. Boy, was I in for a surprise.

A few weeks after the video went live, emails started slowly trickling in with questions about residency. I came back to Mexico after Christmas break ready to hit the ground running with appointments for clients. In just a short time, I went from helping a few people here and there fill out their immigration paperwork, to starting to have a full-fledged client base.

I had learned about a WhatsApp group focused on immigration help in CDMX, so I joined it, hoping to provide my knowledge and services to potential clients and learn more about the various procedures people need assistance with. I would regularly engage and answer questions - but was quickly removed from the group by the admin for what I learned was not being a "vetted partner."

I was disheartened and felt a little defeated until I got a private message from another member of the group encouraging me to start my own WhatsApp group focused on residency. She felt my contributions were really the only ones that had any depth to them and would be the first person to join my group. So I did it. Two and a half years later, our group has hit over 750 members and grows daily.

I decided to make the business a little more official by creating a *Facebook* page encompassing basically all things that I do, education, immigration, relocation, and more. I kept doing my work and eventually had to hire an assistant. For me, it was imperative that I created jobs for Mexicans, and therefore hired a trilingual college student studying politics and public administration. Perfect fit.

Shortly thereafter, I was contacted by the publisher of a major resource for all things Mexico relocation, asking if she could feature me as her Mexico City preferred facilitator.

Uhm, yes, please!

At this point, my name had spread like wildfire through the foreigner community and I had quickly and fondly become known as DrG. I also decided to take on some outreach of my own, connecting with Risa Marimoto, owner of Dream Retirement International, and another YouTuber, who agreed to do an interview with me. Meanwhile, I was also doing relocation videos with Mexico Relocation Guide, on life in different cities, Specifically focusing on Mexico City and Cuernavaca, the city where it all began for me.

The story of people reaching out repeats itself.

As business got busier, I brought on more Mexican employees, each working as individual contractors, while I started adding on services. I began doing relocation tours, offering "moving in" services: setting up utilities, taking parents to check out schools, apartments, and grocery stores, and even accompanying clients to the store to purchase furniture and appliances. What started as a little side hustle in late 2021 as a move out of desperation turned into a full-fledged agency with five part-time Mexican independent contractors, whose extra income is beyond life-changing for them.

The business hasn't only been life-changing for me or my staff, but also for the clients I work with. Although our clients all have different motives for moving to Mexico, for some of them it's been a lifelong dream, like mine. I've had moments when I questioned my work, having gone from a teacher where you see the daily impact on my students, to managing Mexican bureaucratic procedures for foreigners.

Yet, frequently enough, my clients remind me that I'm changing lives and making dreams come true. I've been affirmed repeatedly by my clients, and every time I learn something new or successfully process a complicated case, I am reminded that what I am doing, is in fact, important.

One of my most challenging cases that really tested my learning curve involved a family of three, a husband from the U.S., his Brazilian wife and mother-in-law, three countries, two consulates, multiple flights, and in the end, a beautiful multicultural family of three happily residing in Mexico. *My favorite part?* The husband's review. I've had many titles and been called many things in life, but an immigration wizard is probably the most entertaining to date!

My business has allowed me freedom that I never could have imagined. Ever since I was a two-year-old girl my favorite phrase (according to my mother) was, "*No, Mommy, I do it myself...*"

And well, what can I say? I have done it.

I spend my spare time volunteering with organizations that align with my passions, education, juvenile justice, and dog rescue. I travel within Mexico as much as possible to learn more about the country, its history, and culture (and to prepare for my naturalization exam in 2025), and to provide as much accurate information to my clients as possible.

I can only hope and dream that we continue to grow, I can continue to support the Mexican economy by creating jobs for people who wouldn't have the opportunity to earn a living wage otherwise, and we can make a difference in the lives of people wanting to relocate to Mexico.

But the work doesn't stop there.

With the business taking off so quickly and most of our client base coming from social media and word of mouth, there was no time to focus on the formalities (we don't even have a *Google* page, much less a website! Thank God for *Facebook* and WhatsApp groups). The important aspect was focusing on the clients.

With the business running smoothly, and a well-established and reliable staff at my side, I have no intentions to stop growing. I continue to build relationships with others in the business, having regional partners and collaborators to bounce ideas off of, gather information, and share knowledge across all of Mexico.

Aside from the residency and relocation, my dream is to grow the educational aspect of the business, teaching people not only about the residency process but also about how to respectfully and responsibly live in Mexico. I hope to give back to my clients through more than just our services, but also by coaching them on all things Mexico, and teaching them how to see and treat Mexico, not only through their eyes, but through mine as well.

AUTHOR
GABRIELLE SMITH

Gabrielle Smith (DrG), is a former high school Spanish teacher and juvenile probation officer. Originally from Arizona, she spent a small portion of her childhood in San Diego where she was first immersed in the Spanish language and Mexican culture through her school friends and weekend jaunts walking across the border to Tijuana.

Always living her life in color, Mexico truly grabbed her by the heartstrings in 2000 when she participated in a Spanish Language Immersion program in Cuernavaca, Mexico where she learned more than just the language. She learned where she belonged.

Over the course of her adult life, she's lived in four U.S. states, Washington, D.C., and now, Mexico City, Mexico.

Some of her favorite things in the world are being Catholic, traveling, the color lime green, dog rescue (including her own, a thirteen-year-old rescue mix born in her closet while she was fostering the mother, and her "Mexican street rat" she picked up outside her daily coffee shop on *Dia de los Muertos* in 2020), reading, writing, and her nephew.

She dreams of writing more, bridging cultural differences, and starting a non-profit to take young adults who have never traveled outside of their hometowns to see the world.

Connect with Gabrielle:

https://www.facebook.com/DrGResidency/

CHAPTER 4: PASSPORT TO PIVOT

By Stephanie Wandke

1. The Beginning: Discovering My Niche

I grew up in a log cabin on the Peshtigo River in the northern woods of Wisconsin. Built with logs floating down the waterway during the heyday of paper making in this town with one stop light, the seventy-year-old, nine-hundred square foot cabin had black logs with white end caps and was heated by only a wood stove. For half the year, it was a perfect winter postcard. The other half of the year, it quickly rotated through the seasons. The grass and trees would bloom, thrive, and then turn into the bright colors of fall until only the tall green pines remained, ready to be blanketed in white once more.

As beautiful and serene as life is inside a postcard, as soon as I was an adult I was looking for a warmer place to live. I almost immediately moved to Los Angeles and quickly fell in love with its palm trees and fast-paced life. I was working eighty hours a week for a really exciting robotic surgery company, spending my days in operating rooms with the daVinci robot and world-famous surgeons. But it didn't take long before I was burnt out and unsatisfied with the constant denial of vacation days and the prospect of doing this every day for forty years.

I wanted a future filled with the images I'd ripped out of Conde Nast Traveler. Plus, I couldn't imagine that I would still want to go on those adventures after retirement and began to wonder if some would even still exist by the time I found the time.

Feeling justified and invincible at the age of twenty-eight, I quit my six-figure salary and planned a year-long trip around the world. This was it, I decided. Instead of waiting for decades, every seven years I would take a one-year mini-retirement to pursue the bucket list items of my choosing and then return to my career with a fresh outlook and deeper meaning.

But as you can imagine, it didn't really turn out that way.

I always meant to return to Intuitive Surgical, or at least my first love of robots, but I ended up falling for the small English-speaking country of Belize in Central America. There my life abroad began without much of a plan. I found true connections in both people and nature and adored their rich culture of giving, community, and deep joy for the present moment. I knew there was a lot I could learn from them, and it was warm. Like super warm.

After a few years of volunteering for everything in our village and singing karaoke with new backpackers every month, I started to get restless and run out of money. Turning north to the Hummingbird Highway, I moved to a wooden house on stilts along a jungle river where I enjoyed endless summers and the sticky humidity of tropical living.

One day I looked out my window at the royal palm trees lining my driveway and the blossoming brilliant orange flamboyant tree. I had found my way back to a postcard, but this time the trees dropped 20-foot palm leaves (loudly) and toucans visited to feast on the cherry red berries adorning the trees around my porch. I couldn't bear to leave this sweet life abroad and needed a way to make money without relinquishing the paradise and lifestyle I had found.

I decided I needed to figure out something I could do online. It was then, nestled within the vibrant jungles of the Maya mountains, that my journey as a digital nomad and entrepreneur began.

My initial idea was simple but ambitious: help tourists find organizations they could volunteer with on their vacations. The first thing a modern business needs is a website, so I turned to *Google* to ask how to do it. I grew up in the nineties taking typing classes and yes even a bit of HTML in high school. After I dusted off that part of my brain and set to work, I was pleasantly surprised to find that I didn't need it and a website could be built without writing a line of code. But as I developed the accompanying business plan, it soon dawned on me that the regulations around working and volunteering abroad are extremely complicated. There are visas, permits, and endless interactions with government offices. Uh, no thank you. I had to come up with something else.

I soon had another idea and started to build a different website. Before too long, I scrapped that idea too. It was not until my third business idea, and third website, that a light bulb went off. The process of creating websites, rather than these business ideas, was where my true interest lay.

And so it was there, surrounded by orchids, banana trees, and toucans, that I decided to start a website business with dial-up internet.

Tucked into the only corner of the house not open to the jungle noises and shielded from rain that often came sideways through the screen-only windows, my "desk" was about as big as a placemat and technically a closet. Simple phone calls over the required VPN took so much bandwidth that I couldn't look at the client's website while talking with them. I would furiously take notes on soggy paper while the tantalizing smells of my boyfriend making fry jacks and beans in our tiny kitchen would distract me.

On most days, the internet just flat-out sucked. I would question this crazy idea of working online from anywhere and wondered when someone was going to figure out that I was a fake. But the clients kept calling and my internet kept getting faster. Just kidding, the internet didn't get faster. But the ability to grow this business while still living in Belize started to feel more real. Filling my spare time with riverside bike rides and midday strolls around my yard to collect bouquets of truly exotic flowers was exactly the lifestyle I wanted to build. I was building.

After so many years of structure and planning, I was now finding success by leaning into my intuition and passions. Finding what works often means trying many different things and following the path that becomes interesting. For me, realizing that I could explore both my creative and technical talents while building websites was as exciting as it was surprising. It wasn't the path I had envisioned, and in almost every way, it was better. I found something that sparked my interest and I could do it from anywhere.

2. The Nomadic Years: Can I Balance Traveling and Working?

After that lightbulb moment in Belize, I realized that anywhere means *anywhere*. I hit the road, with exactly one suitcase and my laptop, diving headfirst into the digital nomad lifestyle. Over the next seven years, my office views ranged from hotel rooftops overlooking the Great Pyramids of Egypt to serene fjords in New Zealand. I was living the dream, crossing off about twenty countries from my bucket list, all while keeping the business afloat.

I take Belize with me everywhere I go (Egypt, 2018).

This period was a Masterclass in Modern Nomad Techniques. Some days, I'd find myself lost in the beauty of a new city, only to scramble for a decent wifi connection minutes before a client call. Others, I'd finish my workday with a local cultural experience or drinks with a friend I met three countries ago and accidentally stay out all night. It was a blend of freedom and discipline, of spontaneous travels and midnight meetings.

In big cities, it was easy to find fast internet, but also easy to get distracted by shiny lights the bevy of enticing restaurants. Small towns had decent connections, but not much to do. And of course nearest the most impressive natural wonders, wifi was still a novelty. You can guess where I kept finding myself.

One of the most remote places I tried to work was from the South Pacific island nation of Vanuatu. My flight from Port Vila to the active volcanic island of Tanna took off on a crystal clear blue day from a runway too large for its tiny body. Me and my laptop were sitting shotgun in a nine-passenger Britten-Norman BN-2 Islander plane with a female pilot, also named Stephanie. I couldn't contain my excitement. I was going to hike to the top of an active volcano, stay in a treehouse, and get some work done during my downtime. This was the ultimate in digital nomad life.

I put on the heavy headset from the seventies and immediately after take-off, I joked to our pilot that she had a great office view, like me. Hers was through this windshield and mine was anywhere with the internet. She laughed and agreed. Within a few minutes, there was nothing but shades of blue in every direction dotted with tiny white clouds above and below us and I suddenly felt quite small and vulnerable. I had been in these small planes dozens of times in Belize, but there was always land nearby and islands everywhere. I nervously asked how long until we arrived. Stephanie said, relax, we have one hour. This did not relax me. I gripped my laptop tighter, then laughed at my absurdity and misaligned priorities.

She expertly landed us on a strip of pavement surrounded by thick jungle overgrown with lush green palms and sweet-smelling hibiscus. We took a quick selfie together and I was waved down by a friendly family with a small red pickup truck. They had been sent by the guesthouse to pick me up. I squished my long legs into the tiny halfback seat and they threw my luggage into the dusty back bed. I kept my laptop close while we shopped for vegetables at the local market.

I made my selection from the coconuts, peanuts, potatoes, and any other thing you can imagine that looks like a coconut or a potato and checked my watch.

I knew we had a bit of a drive and I had some work and meetings this afternoon. We jumped in the truck and after about twenty minutes we took a sharp turn over a large volcanic ash dune. We dropped into an expansive black desert that smelled of smoke and sulfur and turned into the shadows of Mount Yasser volcano. Driving down a narrow black pathway lined with tall leaves and tropical flowers, gorgeous spiked palms slapped the doors and tires as the cab swayed back and forth. It opened into a small clearing with vibrant greens growing in every direction and a magnificent 80 ft tree with my room nestled about halfway up.

At this point, the journey had taken a lot longer than I

CHAPTER 4: PASSPORT TO PIVOT | 57

anticipated and I was going to be late for a meeting. I wanted to get this work done so I could explore.

I asked about the Wi-Fi connection and was greeted with a confused look. They pointed to my phone and suggested that the internet was there. I pointed to my laptop and said I would need it here. I also held up the end of my electrical plug, signaling that I'd need to plug into an outlet.

More confused looks.

The middle child ran off to get their cousin who spoke some English. I explained my situation and he informed me that, "*We have wifi,*" which meant that they were one of the few places on the island that could even get a phone signal. I sighed and asked where I could at least plug in.

He shook his head some more. "*No, I'm sorry,*" he said, "*We do not have electricity either!*"

I couldn't help but laugh at where I now found myself. I was so worried about protecting my laptop.

But, what was it without electricity or the Internet? Useless.

I slid my laptop back into my bag. I called my client and explained I was in the shadow of a rumbling volcano without power, then canceled my meetings for the rest of the week.

I actually thought I was going to work from here (Vanuatu, 2020).

It was times like these that I was grateful I was the boss, but also laughed at myself for being a seasoned traveler and still making rookie mistakes. Thankful for my understanding clients, I was now able to be fully present with this volcano. But at what cost?

Traveling while working forced me to become incredibly flexible and efficient but also made me exactly the opposite sometimes. The constant movement, blur of airports, and rotating accommodations took its toll. It is difficult to feel fully present in any activity when you feel like you should be doing another. Days exploring mossy misted waterfall canyons were pierced with the guilt of missing an informative webinar. And when hours turned to days of back-to-back meetings, I'd stare out the window wondering why I'd come so far just to go nowhere.

After seven years, I began to crave something different—a balance that allowed me to savor my surroundings without the looming pressure of the next meeting. Maybe it was time to reevaluate and reshape my nomadic lifestyle.

3. The Pivot: It's Not Paradise if You're Stuck

I had been living in Tasmania, Australia, balancing the digital nomad and entrepreneurial dream, when I took that trip to Vanuatu. While there, I learned that just west, the diving was better and the internet speeds first class. So in March of 2020, when I needed to leave Aussie to reset my tourist visa, I booked a dive trip to New Caledonia. Little did I know, that decision to take a small diving trip would turn into my life's biggest detour.

Just two days after landing in Noumea, the borders of this French island territory closed along with the rest of the world. What was supposed to be a few weeks and then a few months morphed into a year-long stay on a remote island in the South Pacific.

After a strict early lockdown, we lived a relatively normal life, except I was trapped on an island where I didn't speak the language and everything was astronomically expensive. I saw a billboard advertising a Big Mac Meal for $39 USD.

At first, the language barrier felt like a wall. Not only was everyone French speaking but when they warned of the borders closing, all other tourists left. I downloaded Duolingo and unlocked Owl achievements daily, but then I would go out in real life and manage to squeeze French, English, and a splash of Spanish into one sentence. It left me feeling vulnerable and frustrated and I spent a lot of time alone in my hotel room.

But as days turned into months, those feelings turned into a focused energy that changed my entrepreneurial journey. Stranded in paradise, without the usual hustle and bustle of travel, I found there wasn't much else to do but work. The distractions of constant movement were gone, replaced by a level of commitment and clarity I hadn't realized I was missing.

During this time, I doubled down on my business. I hired a coach, built a team, and landed some important and complex projects with impressive clients. It was a period of intense growth, both for my business and for me personally. This unexpected pause made me realize that the energy I'd been pouring into my travel addiction could be redirected into building something lasting. I started seeing my business—and myself—in a new light.

4. The Realization: Dream Life is Real Life

This shift in perspective was transformative. I needed to find a place to live next that could balance my love for exploration and travel yet I could ground myself within a connected community. After much thought, I decided to move to Merida, Mexico, a place I had visited often when living in Belize. I was conversational in Spanish and correctly guessed it would be a place many of my friends and family from Belize, the U.S., and Europe could visit easily.

I arrived in early 2021, and as soon as I landed I started joining local *Facebook* digital nomad groups. There were regular meetups and almost immediately I met other adventurous and intelligent entrepreneurs that shared so many of my ideas and values. It allowed me to tap into a deep network of successful friends, a community that has become a source of inspiration, collaboration, and support.

It also didn't take long for me to realize the luxury of living near an international airport that could quickly carry me almost anywhere in the world. My first trip after settling into Merida was a two-week journey around Austria and a week of Fatboy Slim and Pete Tong shows in the U.K. with my sister. For the first time in a decade, I was able to confidentially travel without deadlines and enjoy the perks of being offline without worry. This balance of stability and adventure has enriched my life in ways I hadn't anticipated but was always yearning for.

Looking back on my journey—from the early days of website flipping in Belize to finding my footing on a remote island in New Caledonia, and finally finding a rhythm in Mexico that blends travel with stability—I've come a long way. Each chapter of my story has been filled with invaluable lessons, not just about business, but about life itself. I've learned the art of adaptability, the strength found in community, and the importance of carving out a path that resonates with my deepest values and self.

I've come to understand that for me, the essence of true success lies in aligning my work and lifestyle, ensuring that each enriches the other. This harmony has allowed me to live my dream of exploring the world while providing value through my work and building stronger relationships, both personally and professionally.

Home (Merida, 2023).

For those embarking on their journey as digital nomads or entrepreneurs, I offer this advice: embrace flexibility and be open to change. The road to finding your niche or your ideal way of working is rarely straight and often long. It's filled with twists, turns, and unexpected detours that will guide you to exactly the right destination. Remember they are not setbacks but opportunities to grow and refine your dream life.

As the possibilities of remote work expand, I'm encouraged by the number of people I meet who are looking for a way to live a more authentic life. I see a future where the borders between work and personal pursuits blur and where people are empowered to design their lives around both their passions and professional ambitions.

My hope is for you to have the bravery to take the first step.

Abroad.

AUTHOR
STEPHANIE WANDKE

Stephanie Wandke is a biomedical engineer turned entrepreneur in pursuit of a more perfect union of life and work. She left her career and the US at twenty-eight to depart on an around-the-world trip before the advent of wifi and smartphones. A complete immersion in cultures and present moments resulted in a radical mind shift and the desire to live abroad and continue the journey.

In 2013 she started her marketing and website agency and has found immense joy in empowering clients while partnering with other female entrepreneurs around the world. Her latest interests in AI will certainly fuel her next wave of endeavors and interests.

When not working, she is fire dancing, practicing yoga, building miniature scenes, painting with glitter, or enjoying nature with friends. The best days are when she's doing it all at once.

She is proud to live a life that is full of curiosity, fun, and freedom surrounded by people who inspire, love, and create.

Connect with her at:

https://www.stephaniewandke.com

CHAPTER 5: AFAR

By Casey Hearne

Have you ever wondered what it would be like to live abroad?

Far from everything that you know, everything you have ever really known. I used to wonder. Every single time we went on a family vacation growing up, I wondered.

What would it be like to live in a cold, snowy, ski town? What would life be like? Full of snowballs and hot cocoa? What would it be like to live at the beach?

I think we took more trips to cold climates. Probably, because our starting point, Texas, is generally a warm place and if any snow does come, it's very little.

I remember going skiing. It is a very trying sport, honestly. Just like anything else, I know it gets easier with practice. For me, however, it would take me a couple of days to get over the fear of the mountains to actually put on some snow boots and click them into the sky on the way up the mountain. *What a rush!*

With the beach, what is there? Surfing! The complete opposite of skiing. Only because of the climate difference.

Every trip, I feel like I got a little bit deeper. Deeper into the experience. Deeper into imagining what it would actually be like to just stay in one of these towns with a beautiful vibe and gorgeous, vibrant scenery. From colorful Colorado mountains and lakes to the sun-dried clay bricks mixed with grass to build homes and moccasin shoes made by the native tribes in New Mexico to the delicious flavors of handmade salsa and tortilla chips in Mexico to many states and then all the way to Europe!

After a while though, you just start to wonder what else is out there. *Why revisit a place when there are so many other places out in the world to explore?* To witness them before it's too late... Set your eyes on them and experience all of their culture before there are too many tourists to blind your way.

My name is Casey Hearne. I grew up in Arlington, Texas. It's right in between the famous cities of Dallas and Fort Worth. My first big move was to Austin, the music capital of the world! That's right. Austin, Texas baby. I love that city! After Austin, I moved to Hawaii... Oh, that was before Austin. Then, I moved to California to tag along with my big brother Cole. We both had always had dreams of moving out of Texas.

Well, we did it! This was HUGE!

After he passed, I ended up back in the Austin area and then flurried off to Colorado. The winter was coming! *Yew! Got out of there just in time!*

El Salvador

Central America was calling. Now, I have my home base in El Salvador where I host wellness and surf retreats with some friends. I may have found a home base but my heart yearns to learn more and see more. I always wanted a travel partner.

For years, it was always me and some friends or a friend and always someone different it seems like. I just wanted one person to continue my travels... Someone to say, *"Remember when?"* with. A lot of death has crept through the scenes in my book, which in retrospect makes one realize how short life really is. We always think there will be tomorrow but there is NO guarantee.

I am going to tell you a little about what it is like to actually live abroad. Things that people may not always talk about.

Learning Spanish

When I first came to Central America, I knew little Spanish. As in, I worked in restaurants in Texas and there were always Latin men working in the kitchen. I had them teach me a word a day for a while, but the majority of my Spanish-speaking knowledge was about kitchen supplies and food. I only knew how to say, "¡Hola! ¿Cómo estás? ¿Dónde está el baño? (the most important one, obviously) and "¿Qué pasó?"

Funny little details we find out way deeper into learning a second language. I came here and could not even understand or remember how to ask, "*How much is it?*" That's the one thing that really was hard for me to grasp. I took ten Spanish classes after arriving in El Salvador. I took my little notebook and an English/Spanish dictionary around with me everywhere and would say, "*Un momento, por favor,*" and take the time to look up every word I was trying to say. People were patient with me. Very patient if you can imagine trying to complete a full sentence one word at a time.

I used to go to the beach and hang out with all of the surfer dudes until I would realize I had no idea what they were talking about and they could have been talking about me for all I knew. I would suddenly get up to go home and they would say, "*tranquila*" which means relax. Then, I would remember that I wasn't in the States anymore and really didn't have any need to rush anywhere. There's no rush hour traffic when you're walking everywhere you go. However, sometimes it does take a while to get down the street if you stop and talk to everyone who greets you on your route. I'd never seen so many friendly people before in my life.

La piedra, the rock, at El Tunco beach in El Salvador.

Anyway, I studied hard. The hostel I lived in had a three-year-old who lived there and she taught me more than anyone I can give credit to. She had, and still has, no problem correcting me when I'm wrong with my Spanish. *Who knew that children could teach us so much!?*

I applaud myself for going barefoot and grounding myself, becoming one with the Earth. I was extremely proud of myself when I made it a full month without shoes! Eventually, I stubbed my toe on a rock and had to start wearing sandals again so it would heal.

Oh right, back to learning Spanish.

One day, I looked around and noticed there were no more English speakers here. Now, I understand that means the busy season was over and the rainy season is coming. I had no choice but to learn at this point. Make it or break it.

I could sit there and guess what people were saying and wondering if they might be talking about me or laughing at me for something silly. I certainly didn't fit in here at first.

Cultural Differences

Here are some examples of cultural differences living abroad.

I felt weird at the beach at times because we were the only ones with swimsuits and didn't just swim in shorts and a t-shirt or a dress or whatever attire we had on for the day. It makes one doubt whether we should take off clothes off and expose our swimsuits.

That reminds me of a time I went to Happy Hallows at the lake in Austin. I saw a sign, had no idea what it was, and I went there with my dog. A fully dressed man asked if he could sit with us and I said sure. Little did I know he was about to strip down butt naked and plop down next to us. I remember, plain as day, I was lying there writing in my journal. I think I even wrote about this situation! *Haha!* I noticed he had a ring around his penis. It looked like the ring on a condom. What an awkward way to break in a gal to a nudist lake site! What a wild experience!

That's a great example of what I am attempting to describe here. Feeling completely out of place, frozen, and speechless. It's also a funny feeling being the only white person in sight. I understand how minorities feel. I am in the minority. "*All eyes on you kid.*" Everywhere I went, everyone was looking at me. It still happens, but, now I know a lot of people so it usually comes with a friendly hello.

Coming from the first world to a developing world is a leap of action in itself. I think smartphones had just come out but not *Google* Maps yet when I moved here. People here barely knew how to text when I came. The Internet barely existed and there most certainly wasn't wifi anywhere. It was like going back in time. Which was great for me. Unconnected and getting away from the hustle and bustle.

We put the toilet paper in the trash can here. Our plumbing cannot handle it. Most of the public bathrooms don't have toilet paper and you are lucky if they have running water to flush the toilet when you are done doing your business. Huge water catchers/large trash can-looking things are filled with water and a small bucket is left inside for you to dump water in the toilet when you are done. The weight of the water naturally flushes the toilet. *Who knew?* You can just pour water right into the toilet bowl.

Bathtubs are pretty much non-existent in developing countries. Processed foods are barely seen and if they are they are found in the import section of the grocery store. Pick-up trucks drive around to towns to offer a variety of colorful fruits and vegetables. Women walk around with baskets on their heads with fresh baked goods like tamales and all kinds of other delicious treats. There's a bicycle that rolls through the neighborhood in the wee hours of the morning tooting its horn. *Pan!* Fresh French bread that is! In the afternoon, another bike comes around blowing its horn with warm, fresh-out-of-the-oven sweet bread. Public transportation is the main form of transportation and you can get from one end of the country to the other with probably $5 after interchanging buses.

Women and children walk for miles with buckets on their heads to bring water home to their families. It's a beautiful change of pace for anyone from the U.S. Some of the older citizens are way more healthy than anyone half their age in the States. Mainly from walking miles but also using machetes to open fresh coconuts or chopping plants to clear a walking path off of the main street.

It's inspiring to see how people live off of the land. I had always dreamed of living off of the land and growing my own food. I grow a lot of my own food these days which says a lot for someone who could barely keep a plant alive in my younger years.

There's so much to learn while traveling abroad. You also meet other travelers who will tell you about more places that are a "must-visit" making the list of never-ending destinations even longer.

Most people here do not have air conditioning. I don't as a matter of fact. We live in a tree house with a palm leaf roof and a fan attached to the wall. It's the most amazing thing to me. I love this place that I've grown to call home. It's quite different from where I came from which obviously makes it more intriguing for me to stay to experience the world in a different way, a more humbled way away from the materialistic jargon of first-world society.

People use plant medicine first and foremost. Most of the country can't afford a doctor's visit if they need one. *Why would they need to anyway if they can cure themselves from their yard?* I think Big Pharma and other fancy-named jerks have robbed us of our birthright and abilities to be able to cure ourselves from mental and plant medicinal practices.

Raising a Child Abroad

Thankfully, I did finally find someone to say, *"Remember when we were in _____ and such and such happened?"* with. A beautiful baby boy was born on July 15, 2016, named Esteban Marley. That boy is my son. This kid changed my life and most certainly changed my future.

Esteban playing at the beach near our home.

But most importantly, he became someone to travel with me and always be by my side to say, *"Remember when..."* I'm grateful for him and our time together, although I know he will eventually find his own travel partner one day and venture off into the sunset with her. Until that day, I will cherish him walking by my side watching these memories from our worldly adventures that constantly pop up.

There are many obstacles to raising a child living abroad. It can be challenging at times. We want our children to be properly educated. At times it can be hard trying to raise children with good values such as not throwing garbage out the car window like many Salvadoreans do.

The country was divided after the war in the 1980s and many people were not educated during this time. The generation my parents grew up in, the baby boomers, mainly, did not learn to read or write. This is a huge difference. Many things were not taught in the educational system. Littering is a big one.

Taking care of automobiles is another big pollution factor that we don't want our children to follow. There is no system in place to not let public buses or personal vehicles blow black smoke out of their exhaust pipes.

Finding a bilingual school can be challenging. We live at the beach, and there are not many close by. Esteban's first language to learn was Spanish. He later learned to speak English. Teaching children to know the difference between a normal-priced service vs. *gringo* pricing is a big thing too. Those with white skin who are not aware of the going rate for a service can easily be swindled. These are all important subjects to teach your children.

We speak both English and Spanish at home. It's great that we are submerged in a Spanish-speaking culture making Esteban suck Spanish in like a sponge. He will have better opportunities for his future with one step ahead already speaking two languages.

Learning to navigate bathrooms is another biggie. Here, it is good to always carry toilet paper because many times public restrooms do not have them. Teaching children which water is safe to drink is a huge task in itself. Explaining to Esteban that the water system is different and the water that comes from the faucet is filled with parasites and not clean enough to drink.

Our town, recently, built a septic system to cleanse the dirty toilet water. The system has not been perfected yet and most homes, previously, had sewage pipes (and many still do) that release sewage into the rivers. Teaching our children not to play in the river water or by the river mouth where the river meets the ocean.

On the upside, the children here still play in the streets and ride bikes around the neighborhood for fun. We also have the sand and ocean at a moment's walk. Most kids don't even need toys if they can build sandcastles in the sand and jump in the waves.

Traveling abroad is a brave and oh-so-rewarding accomplishment to have under your belt. If you've ever dreamed of it, you should try it. *What's the worst that could happen?* You don't like it and return to your starting point. *Doesn't sound so bad, does it?*

With all of the rewarding experiences to be had and lessons to be learned, I suggest everyone go on at least one trip abroad at some point in life. You'll definitely learn a lot and maybe find out some things about yourself that you never even knew. This life is short. Don't spend it waiting for that "eventually" or "one day". Go out there and make your dreams a reality!

Who knows, maybe you'll end up writing a book about your experiences just like me.

AUTHOR CASEY HEARNE

Casey was born and raised in Arlington, Texas USA. She and her son, Esteban, have been traveling the world as often as possible to teach Esteban about different cultures and the history of Mother Earth as a whole.

Casey is an eight-time published author, has three yoga teaching certifications, a meditation certification, and is a Reiki Master.

She, also, gives tours to waterfalls, hot springs, volcanoes, lakes, and many other great spots in the quickly growing community of El Salvador. She has a food truck that serves delicious vegetarian and vegan meals. They also rent rooms to travelers from around the globe.

She has been living in Central America for thirteen years and has adapted to the lifestyle changes quite well. The thought of returning to the United States is very hard to grasp after living abroad for such a long time. Her son would not have the same quality of life if they were to return. They are settled in, for now, until something more exciting comes their way.

Until then, Sunshine Yoga And Surf Retreats will remain located on the Pacific Coast of El Salvador where the ocean is warm and waves are plentiful for surfing, tropical fruits and local produce are in abundance, and dishes are made from scratch.

Look it up to book your getaway and come soak in the sun and let your worries melt away in a tropical paradise where you can sip fresh coconuts as often as you please. Or just follow along with their adventures. A sunny adventure awaits.

They can be reached on *Instagram* and *Facebook*: @SunshineYogaRetreats @Sunshiney14U

WhatsApp: +503-7563-6594

*Many thanks to Sara for all of the inspiration
and love put into the books.*

CHAPTER 6: LIVE OUTSIDE YOUR COMFORT ZONE

By Sara Tyler

Take a second and think of the people you spend most of your time around. They are probably your significant other, children, extended family, neighbors, and co-workers.

Now, ask yourself honestly: *Do these people look, sound, and think like you? Are they the same race? Same nationality? Do you belong to the same economic class? Political party? Religion?*

Most Americans will answer yes to these questions because most of us stay in the general area where we grew up. And this is our original comfort zone. This is where I lived for the first twenty-four years of my life, too.

The vast majority of us grow up surrounded by our family and friends, who share the same language, culture, values, religion, educational backgrounds, and socio-economic status.

The people around us influence every part of our lives, including friendships, romantic relationships, educational and employment opportunities, physical and mental health, and even financial decisions.

For better or for worse.

And in my case, my environment in the U.S. was definitely worse.

Traveling Abroad Opened My Eyes

I grew up in a small town in the United States and my family didn't have money. Our summer vacations were always to the same place, to the Jersey Shore, because a wealthy uncle owned a beach house there and let us stay for free. Otherwise, we wouldn't have been able to afford to go on vacation.

I never dreamt of traveling because, in my mind, that was just something that rich people did. In fact, I didn't really dream of anything. For as long as I can remember, I just wanted to work. I took after my dad in that way. He worked sixty-hour weeks for as long as I can remember and money was still always tight. No one complained when I dropped out of high school and started working full-time because that meant that I could pay rent and contribute financially to our household.

Like many low-income families, I grew up around a lot of alcohol and drugs. In high school, Xanax and painkillers were becoming popular and it seemed like everyone had a prescription for them. But no one had more prescriptions than my mother. She had carpal tunnel syndrome and somehow was prescribed painkillers usually given to terminal cancer patients. It was normal for me that people would share and trade their pills, or mix alcohol with Xanax so it hits harder because that's the environment that I was brought up in.

I didn't know it at the time, but my environment, my comfort zone, was limiting my life in ways that I couldn't even imagine. I wish I could say that I saw this for myself and took steps to change it, but it didn't happen that way. It was just luck that I had the opportunity to travel abroad and see how much more to life there was.

Throughout high school, I had an older boyfriend, who had a car and his own apartment, so I lived more like a young adult on my own than a typical high school student. We regularly took day trips to places like Washington, D.C., and the beach. Then, for my 18th birthday, he wanted to take me somewhere special. A co-worker of his had just gotten back from Cancun and couldn't stop talking about how amazing, and cheap, it was.

We hopped on the internet and started researching. Sure enough, we found a hotel on the beach in the Cancun hotel zone for less than $40 a night (this was 2004 for reference).

Why the hell were we paying $150+ a night to stay in outdated motel rooms at the Jersey Shore when we could be on a gorgeous, white sand beach in Mexico?

The math was almost too good to be true. Even with first-time passports and flights, we convinced ourselves that we were saving money by going to Cancun instead of the Jersey Shore for vacation.

That first trip to Cancun was the best week of my life up until then. I didn't know that sand could be that white, or the ocean could be that transparent and blue, or that margaritas could be so cheap! Not to mention how friendly and social everyone was - a stark contrast from Philadelphia, where we were from.

We met other travelers who had been all over the world for the first time in my life. I was the first person in my family to even get a passport, so I didn't have anyone in my daily life who knew about these things. That's the danger of staying inside your comfort zone, your hometown environment, where everyone has had the same experiences in life. There's no one to teach you about all the possibilities out there.

The next six years of my life were spent traveling as much as I could afford (and sometimes couldn't afford) with friends, and eventually by myself. I came back to Cancun, Mexico so many times that I started to make friends with hotel staff. We would keep in touch between trips and when I came back, they would take me to downtown Cancun (real Mexico) where I would try authentic Mexican food, drink lots of tequila shots, and listen to live music in Spanish.

Unfortunately, when I was twenty years old, my older brother passed away from an overdose of Xanax. He was the first victim of the environment I grew up in. By this time, I had enough experiences with my significant others' families to realize that the way pills were casually distributed at home wasn't normal. And like unexpected deaths often do, this made me really see how short life can be and only strengthened my interest in spending time abroad.

So, I kept going. With each international trip, I became more and more confident as a solo traveler and eventually would visit Bermuda, Hawaii, Colombia, Guatemala, El Salvador, Honduras, Nicaragua, Costa Rica, and Panama on my own. I didn't worry about being on my own because I would always make friends wherever I went, both other travelers and locals. It was those conversations that I had while traveling that really opened my eyes up to so many different ways to live.

The more time I spent abroad, the more limited I felt when I returned home. My comfort zone was no longer comforting me. It was supposed to be safe, familiar, and predictable, but I felt overwhelmingly bored and uninspired.

It was like I had opened Pandora's box.

Moving Outside of My Comfort Zone

Back home, I found it harder and harder to relate to my friends and family. I had been on all these incredible, once-in-a-lifetime experiences, and they hadn't. Sure, I would try to explain it to them, and they were nice enough to listen, but they didn't get it. And then I started talking about moving abroad, to Mexico, and they *really* didn't get it.

What's wrong with you? Don't you know all the Mexicans want to come here?

Why would you move to a third-world country? It's too dangerous!

Mexico is full of gangs and drugs. You are going to get raped/kidnapped/murdered!

I could go on and on, but I think you get the point. They basically parroted everything negative they heard on Fox News.

The thing is, I had traveled to Mexico at least fifteen times by this point, not just to Cancun but also to Cuernavaca and Mexico City, and knew that what was reported on the news in the U.S. wasn't even close to the truth. The backlash over my move caused many fights, a lot of crying on the part of my mom, and stress in the months leading up to the move.

And that's when I had an *a-ha* moment.

Why would I listen to people who had never been to Mexico, or any foreign country for that matter, themselves?

Or more to the point: *Why would I listen to people who weren't where I wanted to be in life?*

I love my family and friends, but I felt like I had outgrown them at that moment. That I had learned all that I would ever learn from the environment I had grown up in. It was time for something new.

And I made the right decision because within a couple of years, my dad unexpectedly overdosed on prescription pills, and my mom followed him a few years later. Those were victims two and three. My immediate family had really disappeared within a few short years.

I didn't want to end up like them. Not just that they overdosed and died very young and unexpectedly. But also that all those years of my dad working sixty-hour weeks and rarely spending time with us at home had been for nothing because we were always struggling financially.

I wanted something different for my life, so I knew that I had to do things differently.

I moved to Guadalajara, Mexico in 2010, and started a six-week, in-person TEFL diploma program. From my research, I learned that teaching English was a popular, and well-paid, job for expats, so it was a natural choice. I was already majoring in ESL for my degree, but I didn't want to wait four more years to move abroad, so the TEFL diploma gave me credentials for teaching opportunities while I was finishing my degree online.

I wasn't sure if I would like living in Mexico, so I had bought a return flight six months later just in case it didn't work out for me. I only had a couple thousand dollars, from my tax return, to live off of until I started teaching, which also worried me.

But, luckily, I *loved* living in Mexico.

It was a completely different world from the U.S. in so many ways. In Pennsylvania, I worked two jobs, averaging fifty-five to sixty hours a week and another ten hours just commuting, so I was burnt out. But, even I couldn't afford even a basic, studio apartment on my own. In Guadalajara, I rented a furnished room in a posada in downtown, historic Guadalajara, with a shared kitchen for under $300 USD a month. When I moved to Mexico City for work, my rent was even cheaper at $125 USD for a six-month contract.

Teaching part-time at language schools and in companies gave me enough income to support myself living abroad. That meant that I had time to explore, practice Spanish, work out, and really focus on my college courses and assignments for the first time.

Expat life felt like a *real* life, like how a life should be, not just working to pay bills before I die.

Reinventing Myself Over and Over

There is a certain type of freedom that I experienced when I became an expat. I was literally starting over from scratch in a city of twenty-five million people, in a foreign country, with no friends or family to rely on. But, I realized something.

This was the first time in my life that I was 100% in control of *everything*. I didn't have any outside influences or opinions to worry about or any preconceived notions. Since I was little, most of the decisions that I made were based on what someone else thought would be best for me. First my parents, then my older brothers, and finally my boyfriends. Females are brought up to be passive, agreeable, quiet, and to rely on men. Now, I found myself for the first time, relying on myself.

What job do I want to take?
What city do I want to move to?
What type of people do I want to let into my life?

What came next was a period of extreme personal growth as an expat. I physically moved around, living in Veracruz, Cancun, San Salvador (El Salvador), Leon (Nicaragua), back to Mexico in Progreso, Veracruz (again!), Playa del Carmen, Chelem, and Veracruz (third times a charm!), which has been my home base since 2022.

The more places I went, the more people I met. People who were lightyears ahead of me and who were where I wanted to be in life. And just like any environment, they influenced my future, my decisions, and both personal and professional opportunities.

Looking back, I see how far I have come:

First, I was an international traveler.
And then I became a solo female traveler.
And then an expat.
And then a digital nomad.

And then a single mom digital nomad.

And now an expat mom and partner who is worldschooling two little girls.

Moving abroad and taking a chance on this expat life allowed me to change my environment over and over again until I found what really worked for me, without any outside influence. With each move, I reinvented myself each time with a little bit more confidence and freedom than the time before.

My partner, daughters, and I have settled down in Boca del Rio, Veracruz, where we are renovating our house. We have the freedom with both remote, flexible work, and worldschooling to pick up and travel whenever we feel like it - which is often. We take plenty of trips, driving out to the Riviera Maya and Yucatan a couple of times a year, and exploring new cities and states while camping all over Mexico as well. We have built a life based on our common values, beliefs, and goals, which include traveling, educating our girls, and spending quality time as a family.

Being in control of my life abroad as an expat has also influenced me professionally. I have used the same strategy of prioritizing my values to guide me professionally as well. In addition to publishing books written by travelers, digital nomads, and expats (like the one you are reading now), I have been a language teacher since arriving in Mexico in 2010. I use my expat experiences to guide me professionally, teaching both English and Spanish to students who live abroad and need to learn to speak as soon as possible. I also take the activities I do every day with my own bilingual daughters and turn them into language-learning materials, books, and courses meant for other expat families.

Why We Prefer Living in Mexico

It wasn't just the crappy environment that I was raised in that made me want to move abroad. And I don't stay in Mexico because most of my family has passed away. I wanted to move abroad back then and I want to keep living abroad now for so many reasons.

Mexican culture aligns much more with the type of values that I have come to prioritize as an adult. I love the emphasis on family and kids are welcome everywhere you go. This is one of the main reasons I came back to Mexico as a single mom. I knew I would be able to bring my daughter everywhere I went and that people would show her love and affection (and they did!).

I don't want to bring my children to live in the U.S. either because I feel that a large part of the economy is really just a debt trap designed to keep employees working until retirement age. This starts as soon as you become a legal adult with student loans that charge interest - making it that much harder to pay them off. Not only is higher education much more affordable here (the local university charges only a couple hundred dollars total for all the classes for an entire semester) but there are many vocational programs in specialized high schools so students can learn what they want and graduate high school with professional credentials and a career.

Another example is that, in the U.S., it's standard to get a thirty-year mortgage if you want to buy a home (and now there are even thirty-five and forty-year ones). In Mexico, mortgages are extremely rare and if you manage to get one, the interest rates are well over 10%. So, many people buy land instead and build new rooms when they have the money to afford it. There is no need to take on a lifetime of debt to own a home here.

Credit cards are also less common, much harder to qualify for, and with high-interest rates. As a result, people don't fall into a bad habit of buying things they don't need on credit. Instead, they learn to save their money for big purchases, take care of their possessions so they last and will try to fix things before throwing them away or replacing them. What I see here is that people are happier with less material possessions.

And lastly, I want them to be inspired by the entrepreneurs and small business owners that we see all around us here. Growing up,

I never knew anyone who had their own business. Everyone was an employee working for someone else. And just the start-up costs and requirements for potential small business owners in the U.S. put it out of reach for many aspiring entrepreneurs.

But here in Mexico, most businesses can be started without any red tape, so neighborhoods are typically filled with a variety of family-run mom-and-pop stores. We avoid shopping at Walmart, Costco, and other big-name stores and try to spend money at businesses in our own neighborhood. Not only are the mom-and-pop shops less expensive, but I like to support my neighbors and the micro-economies that you find in every *colonia* here. In any given week, we visit and spend money at our local produce stand, butcher, corner store, tortilla shop, bakery, print shop, stationery store, laundry services, and of course, all the taco stands and restaurants people have started in the front room of their homes. These are all within walking distance of our house.

Entrepreneurship is much more accessible to the average person, especially the convenience and financial benefit of operating it out of a property that you already own. Many are also family-run, so you will often see parents taking care of their little kids in their shops (as opposed to going to work and sending children to daycare) which goes back to the importance of family in Mexican culture.

I could go on and on about why we prefer living in Mexico. But my overall point is that we don't just live here because it has a lower cost of living and American dollars go further here. It's a perk to be able to work online and make more than local wages pay, but it's so much more than that.

Our Lifestyle in Mexico vs. the U.S.

I feel like the United States prioritizes money over people. Our government is corrupt and controlled by the richest corporations. Laws and regulations are passed that benefit them, instead of the average American. So, the gap between the rich and the poor is widening and the middle class is disappearing. Companies post record profits every year but don't want to pay a livable wage, health insurance premiums, or pensions for their employees.

The effects mean that if we lived in the U.S., our lives would look very different. Both my partner and I would have to work full-time just to cover the basic expenses of rent or a mortgage, health insurance, utilities, and food. We would most likely need one, possibly two, cars, so that means loan payments, insurance, and gasoline. My youngest daughter would have to go to daycare which is a huge added expense. My oldest would have to go to public school for eight hours a day. My husband and I would have to work opposite shifts, sacrificing family time, or pay additional money for before/after school care.

Here in Mexico, we both work part-time and live a comfortable, middle-class life, and can still afford to travel often. We own our own home outright and share one car that we purchased used. We don't feel any pressure to try and impress others by spending money just because we have it. It's just not that type of society here.

Wrapping It Up

Honestly, I can just go on and on when writing about Mexico, as you can see. But, it's time to wrap up this chapter. If you are thinking of becoming an expat, I am going to ask you to ask yourself just one more question:

What if you had the opportunity to change your environment? How would your new environment affect your personality, values, relationships, and personal and professional opportunities?

To me, that's what expat life is.

You leave your comfort zone, start over from scratch, and purposely build a new life *for yourself by yourself* without any outside influences or distractions.

That is true *freedom*.

AUTHOR AND PUBLISHER SARA TYLER

Sara Tyler is a travel-loving expat mom and 8x bestselling author and publisher. She believes travel is essential for mental health and the best education for kids, teens, and adults.
She started Nomad Publishing in 2021 to help aspiring authors share their travel experiences with the world.

She has written for *International Living* about expat life in Mexico and organized TEDxBocadelRio in 2022. Her home base is Boca del Rio, Veracruz, Mexico, with her partner and two young daughters.

Work with Sara as a multi-author book contributor or solo book author.

For more information on publishing services, contact Sara Tyler directly by text message (+52 56 5050 2513) or WhatsApp:

https://wa.me/message/CJRWPOME3VRJD1

CHAPTER 7: OPERATION OVERSEAS

By Stephanie Wandke

The doctor's visit flashed to the front of my mind. A routine visit to see my gynecologist had resulted in an ultrasound and the most unexpected news of all. I had a tumor that had grown exponentially fast and I needed my uterus removed - immediately. I was truly shocked as it was my younger sister who had issues with this organ her entire life. It was she who had to consider a hysterectomy and have invasive surgery every few years.

I stepped out the door of the doctor's office and instead of calling an Uber, like usual, I just kept walking. The streets of Merida, Mexico, were familiar to me and I needed to process the news.

The pastel concrete facades of the homes shine so brightly in the hot sun that I can barely look at them, so my eyes focus on trying to look inside their open doors. Peering in between iron gates, I saw families sitting down for lunch and smelled the carnitas that had been simmering all morning.

Where one window looks into a family, the next reveals

an overgrown jungle of vines, trees, and ancient construction material. I thought about how many generations of families have lived between these walls. Some are still there, and others have moved on.

I was one of those generations that moved on, wasn't I?

Leaving the United States at the age of twenty-eight and am now still abroad, seventeen years later, building and living my life here in Mexico.

Because of that, I had plenty of experience facing doctors' visits in a foreign language. As a matter of fact, I've had the pleasure of being hospitalized and treated well in six different countries.

In 2009, a couple of friends and I flew to Havana and toured the countryside of Cuba. One day on the beach I threw my back out and ended up in a small medical building getting seen and my treatment in fifteen minutes for eight bucks. I don't think they asked my name, but they did warn me sternly not to have alcohol with this medication. As difficult as it was, I refrained from booze for five days and counted the hours until freedom.

In between two hospital visits, I managed to squeeze in a few games of beer pong in Cuba.

One hour after freedom, I was drinking margaritas and playing beer pong wearing a miniature sombrero at an all-inclusive bar on the beach. I spent the day drinking and the night drinking more at the hotel's nightclub. A few hours into our dance party, my face started feeling numb, and different muscles started seizing up.

I turned to my two friends and asked, *"Does my face look funny?"*

To this day Angela and Noa talk about how horrified they were to see their most fun and joyful friend, frowning. They assured me that everything was fine but maybe we should go see a doctor, and they guided me out of the busy thumping club. They found the nearest luggage rack, loaded it up with the hotel lobby couch cushions, and wheeled me out the front door to a taxi and off to the nearest clinic.

The entrance was nondescript, I might have walked past it earlier in the day and not noticed. There were two glass doors that I could barely see through, and we tumbled out of the taxi and pulled the silver door handle open. The attending nurse took a look at the scene and within minutes I was seen by an English-speaking doctor who quickly gave me some fluids, counteracting meds, and a lecture about actually following the doctor's orders and waiting to drink until the previous medication was fully flushed out of my bloodstream. Again, I was saved in fifteen minutes for about ten dollars.

Because of these kinds of experiences, I was confident that the cost would be reasonable and knew there were wonderful doctors across the world.

But, who will help me through this surgery that I'm about to have in a few days? Certainly, my family doesn't have time to fly down here so quickly.

I started making a checklist in my mind, driving me to the procedure, helping me translate, bringing me home, and assisting with post-surgical care. I thought about my group of friends here. Two years ago we were all strangers, and most of us met at *Facebook* group events and later, in WhatsApp groups. Most often, the only commonality was that we were not from here.

Over time, you figure out that not being from here means you were all brave enough to leave there, and that becomes a really big thing to have in common. And as life events unfold, you begin to lean into these new friends like family. You are the ones who show up for each other, cheer and cry together, and truly understand each other's highs and lows of living abroad. I realized that in a short time, I already had many cherished relationships.

But were they the kind of friends I could count on in this situation?

Let's see. I had seen Courtney construct a toilet in minutes for a desperate friend in need with some cardboard, plastic, a sarong, and two car doors so I knew she was in for the weird stuff. My friend Jenita had three teenage boys and a pocket full of witty quips and sass, so I knew she would be good at reeling in my wild side when I tried to do too much post-op. And Lisa had a heart of gold and cake pans in the shape of marijuana leaves so she was an obvious choice as a nurse.

I had only met these gems in the last couple of years, but yes, I believed we could easily go from friends to family this week.

I crossed into the hot sun and continued to walk home as I recalled my first experience with medicine in Mexico. From a young age, my sister Alyssa had mysterious pains, digestion issues, and fatigue. For years she had been visiting doctors with no results, no diagnosis, and no relief. Things had come to a crescendo when doctors started suggesting maybe it was all in her head.

During this time, I was living in Belize and I had been hearing from more and more friends that they were traveling north to Merida for medical care. Two of my best friends had just returned from a week-long visit where they got a full body workup and health scan for under $500 USD. I suggested to my family that we visit and get medical opinions from an entirely new perspective.

After calculating the expenses, the trip for my family and

estimated costs of doctor visits would be much less than the deductible for their self-employed health care insurance, so they took the leap of faith and booked the tickets.

I took a thirteen-hour bus ride north from Belize and my family flew down from Wisconsin to meet me in the colonial capital city of Yucatan. Right away, we were greeted by our medical tourism concierge who assisted in every step of the process. From scheduling appointments, meeting us at each one to guide us to the office, translating, and helping with paperwork, she walked with us each step of the way.

For her first appointment, the doctor arrived about an hour before usual office hours so there would be plenty of time to get to know Alyssa and discuss her concerns. They did as much as they could right in the office, including an ultrasound, but ultimately decided surgery would be necessary to confirm the suspected diagnosis. We brustled at the idea - we were only in town for this - surely we don't have time to wait for surgery. But we were immediately assured it would be scheduled for the next day. My sister ended up being diagnosed with endometriosis by that team and to this day we credit them with finally giving her the diagnosis she needed and essentially saving her life and sanity.

Protesting the cost of healthcare for my sister in Washington, D.C. in 2013. And it's still true today.

I've had accidents, bizarre afflictions, and even been with family in foreign operating rooms. But this was going to be my first time as a patient. The weird thing was that I knew this procedure. I had worked in robotic surgery and had seen this exact surgery hundreds of times. My mind was still swimming, I stumbled through my front door and collapsed on the couch.

Who should I call first? I first connected with my mom and sister and got depths of reassurance love, and support from them. My mom offered to drop everything and try to come down, but I assured her that I believed my friends would be happy to step in. My sister assured me I was in the right place.

I next called my squad. One by one they offered to do it all, and before long I had a driver, patient advocate, translator, post-surgical overnight care, and a WhatsApp group started. I put the phone down and sighed with relief before bursting into tears. The overwhelming amount of gratitude and fear I felt was too much. As the nervous unknowns crept in, I pictured my loved ones cheering me on. I reminded myself that new experiences are actually what I live for, it's a big part of my reason for living abroad and moving so often.

In addition to preparing for my pre and post-surgical care, there were a few other new things I had to complete before the day of surgery, scheduled in just six days. I first had to visit a few different clinics and complete pre-op blood work and testing. In Mexico, you are in charge of your medical records, so at each stop I had to wait for my results and add them to a packet of information that I would share with the medical team.

My procedure was planned to be laparoscopic, so they were not concerned about large amounts of blood loss. However, it is possible that you need to find blood donors that match your blood type before they will proceed with your surgery.

Since I was going to be going to a private hospital with my surgeon, I had to pay cash for the procedure. Paying cash for services is normal outside the U.S. so I wasn't surprised. I needed to wire my surgeon $3,636 USD for her fees and be prepared to pay the hospital and anesthesiologist around $1,000 the morning of the procedure for my overnight stay, services, and supplies. I also had to arrive at the hospital with about $6,000 Mexican pesos ($300 USD) in cash to rent the video tower that was going to be used for the surgical camera. I was in a very fortunate situation where I had $5,000 dollars in cash in a savings account and was able to move forward with everything immediately.

The preparations happened quickly, and on Friday morning when I woke up, the day had arrived. I surprised myself by not being nervous anymore, but excited. My Uber dropped me at the hospital and Courtney met me with a giant smile, sipping on an iced coffee that I could only smell and envy. We hugged and high-fived before turning to the dimly lit check-in lobby. The soft carpeting and overstuffed couches were comforting and helped me relax even more.

I was confident in both my medical team and my chosen family who were walking with me on this journey. I felt welcome and safe.

We walked up to the desk and proceeded to complete our paperwork and pre-op interviews entirely in Spanish. The staff was warm and friendly, smiling with us and asking in English, once in a while, if we were sure about what we were signing. We would assure her then laugh and high-five again. You really would be surprised to know I was about to get surgery.

As a final step, they had Courtney co-sign for me, agreeing to pay the balance of my hospital bill if didn't which ensued in even more giggles from us and questioning looks from the staff. Next, we had to go to the cashier and prepay for my procedure and hospital stay overnight and after the bill was settled I headed up to my private room.

As a budget traveler, I've stayed in many rooms worse than this. It was spacious with a large couch big enough to sleep on and a large private bathroom with a shower, handicap handles, and miniature soaps. I turned on the large TV to watch a Pixar movie in Spanish while we awaited my surgeon.

Dr. M came in looking rested and calm. She gave me a confident smile as she reviewed the process and procedure. I assured her that I already knew all the steps from my time spent working with the da Vinci robot and with that I did have one odd request. *Could she please take lots of pictures for me?* She gave me a funny look and then she and Courtney burst into laughter. Of course, she agreed. *How could she say no to that?*

Soon after the kind nursing staff came in to transfer me to the surgical bed to be wheeled upstairs. It took three of the small Yucatecan staff to move me into the way-too-tiny bed. I have a hard time even finding shoes my size here, so my ankles and feet hanging off the edge gave me a good chuckle and a reminder of where exactly I was in the world.

I took a deep breath and focused on trying to translate what my nurses were chattering about. Of course, that didn't last too long as the chorus of foreign language is my favorite lullaby and soon I drifted off into the land of anesthesia.

As soon as it started it was over, and I awoke to some more friendly faces and softly spoken Spanish. My nurse assured me that the procedure was successful and that I was in good hands. I drifted in and out of consciousness, as one does post-op, and sighed with relief and peace as I listened to the familiar sounds of hospital beeps and *ranchera* music coming from a radio in the distance.

Within a few hours, I was back in my private suite and laughing with Courtney again. Other sweet members of the squad dropped by with food and plants to brighten the room. After the planned overnight stay in the hospital, the next morning I was discharged with my very detailed care instructions.

I was overconfident and feeling quite fine until we started driving and hitting the usual speed bumps and potholes of our city. It was another quick reminder of where I was and what I had ahead of me. Jenita and Lisa were going to take turns spending the night and caring for my wounds and needs over the weekend. This was quite a new step in our friendships - not only was it difficult to ask for help but each of them had to leave their own lives and families to do it.

I arrived at my house and found them already there with food and laughter arranging flowers that had arrived from friends and family around the world. My new family had already settled into the house and started organizing pillows, medication schedules, meals, and responsibilities. I was sent to the fluffy corner of the couch to rest while my house and life were cared for by others. I sat back and watched with a tear in my eye, truly appreciating how special this life is that I'd built.

Just then my phone beeped, and I had a WhatsApp message from my surgeon. She asked how I was settling in at home and sent a couple of cute stickers. I was so thankful and expressed as much to her, and then she sent over a highlight video of my procedure. I was touched by how special the doctor-patient connection is here in Mexico and opened the video. I cheered, I laughed, I cried; I couldn't get any of my friends to watch it.

My squad and I followed my surgeon's post-operative instructions to the letter, and I recovered in about six weeks with no lingering symptoms or problems. Dr. M came to my birthday party the following month, and she is now one of my friends.

I have immense gratitude for the beautiful people in my life who have helped me navigate all my extraordinary medical emergencies in foreign places. Those experiences show me the human compassion we all share and the incredible support systems that exist, sometimes thousands of miles from where we start.

The Yucatan is a special place for my family.

In the same way that being vulnerable results in deeper

connections with others, going through one of life's most vulnerable moments in a foreign place can make a place a home.

I am so grateful for the kind strangers who have become family and for the quality of care I've received in Mexico and beyond. I continue to marvel at the swift diagnosis, scheduling, and affordability of it all—a combination that continues to be unimaginable for my friends and family in the country where I was born.

AUTHOR STEPHANIE WANDKE

Stephanie Wandke is a fungineer who usually takes the path less traveled. She left on a year-long trip in 2007 and still hasn't returned. I'm serious, no matter how far in the future you're reading this, she still hasn't returned.

She continues to live a life in pursuit of adventure, food, and new friends.

She has always been a healthy person but also continues to find herself in foreign emergency rooms. A life of with jungle hikes, remote islands, scuba diving, wild animals, strange foods, and ancient ruins tends to lend itself to mosquito-borne illnesses, infections, decompression sickness, animal bites, parasites, and concussions. She would not be alive if it weren't for the incredible kindness of people she's met along the way.

If you ever meet her IRL, ask about The Turtle Bite.

Choose your favorite way to connect with her at: https://

www.stephaniewandke.com

CHAPTER 8: DREAMERS ARE DOERS

By Hector Grimaldo

It's noon, the 29th of December, 2023 and I'm drunk.

I'm up next on karaoke. I'm singing, *"Hơn Cả Yêu - Đức Phúc"* for my half-Cambodian and half-Vietnamese girlfriend Van Anh in front of sixty BNI members. It's VIVA's 4th birthday and we are celebrating!

BNI stands for Business Network International, the biggest business network in the world. Vietnam happens to be the second country with the most members in the world. I've been a Member of the platinum chapter of VIVA in Long Bien district in Hanoi, Vietnam for over two years now. And I just taught my BNI family how to shotgun an American beer!

When could I have ever imagined doing something like that as someone who was born into a regular family in Saltillo, Coahuila Mexico?

Those, *"How did I get myself into this situation?"* or *"What am I doing here? How did I get here?"* moments. These are those eureka moments and one of the million reasons why I choose to live abroad. Every day is different and full of surprises and curious situations that seem surreal, like being in a movie or something like that.

When could I have ever dreamt of something like that happening while I was working my nine-to-five at All-State in El Paso, Texas, U.S.A?

When could I have planned a ten-day motorcycle trip across Ha Giang, Vietnam with my best friends for the Lunar New Year holiday just because?

When could I have ever dreamt of speaking Vietnamese fluently?

When would I have ever thought I would have had an impact on more than 10,000 Vietnamese student's lives throughout my education career in Hanoi so far?

When could I have ever dreamt of traveling to 32 countries by the age of thirty-one?

When could I have ever thought that I would be the founder of not one, but two education startups?

After eight years of living in Asia, I like thinking of Dreamland English and Link Online Learners as some kind of energy, karma of all my optimism, positivity, and exchange for tirelessly working and dedicating my time towards trying to build my dream of living abroad.

The result of that energy and frequency waves resulted in the universe manifesting these 2 projects for me. I am proud to stand as the director of Dreamland English and Link Online Learners, but also I stand amazed and baffled.

I used to work at Subway, ended up working in a casino in Michigan, joined the Disney College Program in 2013, suffered through Black Friday as a Best Buy employee, moved into insurance, and studied business at the university.

Even though my mother was a teacher for forty years, and many of my aunts and uncles also worked in education during their lives, I would have never guessed I'd end up in education. This was mostly because I never really decided that I was going to pursue this career. It just *happened.*

I deviated from the standard life tracks of what was expected and boarded my own train, moving towards an unknown destination. Yes, maybe terrifying come to think of it. But, I preferred seeing it as accelerating and thrilling. I enjoyed every single moment in that journey that led me to find what I love doing, and what I am best at. Thinking creatively, public speaking, motivation, teamwork, the exchange of ideas, project management, innovation, and technology.

No university counselor could have suggested a better course of action for me, no personality test could have helped me realize my potential. It was life and destiny itself that brought me to the exact place I needed to be, crossed my path with others I needed to learn and grow from, and also saw me fail and grow frustrated as I went through life's hardships on my own.

I know it sounds corny, but I wouldn't have it any other way now. I have become the man I am today, the digital nomad I can proudly call myself, and the excellent teacher I pride myself in being because of the journey life had in store for me. My dream of traveling the world turned into my career, and it keeps building itself more and more. So much so that it is hard to comprehend sometimes what I have actually done so far.

When could I have ever dreamt of being a voice for education and technology in events in Finland, Estonia, Holland, Germany, Thailand, Vietnam, Kenya, Australia, India, amongst others?

As I'm sharing my story with you, I'm also trying to encourage you. Encourage you to dream, and take that leap. "*Dreamers are Doers,*" I always say. It happens to be the slogan of my school and my TED talk in Hanoi.

Moving on.

My name is Hector Grimaldo. I'm a Mexican/American ed-techpreneur, which means I like working on many different ed-tech projects and start-ups. Funny enough, I believe my upbringing prepared me well for my career.

I'm the proud only child of Jesus Grimaldo Monsivais and Maria De Lourdes Flores. I was born in Saltillo, Coahuila, Mexico in 1992. Due to my dad's job, we moved a ton as a child. We left my hometown when I was four. I started school and I was always the new kid at school, those, *"Hi my name is... Nice to meet you,"* moments built my confidence which led to being able to live my day by having peace and comfort towards myself. Not to mention that I had a positive attitude and joy to live fully, also adding my natural curiosity which came from my mother, who was a teacher for forty years, and father, who even at the age of seventy, keeps up with the latest knowledge in his field.

You could say I had the perfect upbringing to build a digital nomad personality. I could have let the hardships, failures, and embarrassing moments shape me into a negative no-sayer though. I could have clung to excuses and closed up. But I didn't. Not because I'm some kind of prodigy or whatever. It is literally because my optimism does not allow me to be afraid of fear or rejection. I am blinded and engulfed in positivism. Which makes it hard to relate to others who aren't.

These are decisions that could be abided by with a simple, *"Ok, decision. Ok, I'll be positive, OK, I'll try my best today and push forward! Ok, I'll go for it!, What could go wrong, what have I got to lose,"* etc. You get it.

I had finally grown comfortable in Guadalajara, Jalisco Mexico. I had friends and a routine. I was involved in extracurricular activities and clubs, I even had an Xbox 360. Life was great! Then, suddenly, without much warning, my mom and I moved to El Paso, Texas when I was fourteen. There we were in an empty apartment with all the boxes we could fit in the car, sleeping on blankets on the floor.

What had happened? Where am I? Why am I here?

My mom took the leap, the risk I am talking about! She took a chance to give her son a brighter future, without knowing anyone, or anything, without even having a job. She was only thinking of giving me a better future, of giving me more opportunities by improving my English, and by chasing the hope of getting ahead.

Fast forward eight or nine years. There I was graduating from the University of Texas at El Paso, with a BBA in International Business. *Yay!* But also, *yikes!* There I was, frozen by the uncertainty of what came next.

What am I supposed to do now? What should I do? Where should I go? What life do I want for myself? What is even possible? I don't know! Is this what stress is? Is this how others feel?

I could suddenly relate to others when making decisions and overthinking. But that didn't last long. Because I took the most random and out-of-the-box decision ever. Praise the lord for that one couch surfer who stayed with me and told me all about her plan to go to South Korea and teach English as a second language.

Never did I ever think that I would refer to this one talk to make the biggest decision of my life. Never did I ever imagine that she would help shape my life, my dream life, the life I am living now. Thank you, Amanda, wherever you are now!

How Did It Happen?

It wasn't such a random thought of moving abroad for me though. I had dreamt about it before, but that is all it was. Some big dream I didn't know how to turn into a reality. Little did I know, the move to El Paso with my Mom would open the doors to many opportunities.

Disney World, EPCOT, and Mission Space in Florida for an internship in 2013, I was an astronaut taking guests to Mars every day in our attraction.

How did I end up here you ask?

I saw a friend post on *Facebook*, "*I got into the Disney College

Program. OMG!"

So, without any research or much thought, I applied too, and I got it. Not much reasoning behind my decision-making process I know. But these kinds of decisions have led to the best chapters of my life.

Let me give you another example.

My Disney program was coming to an end and I was heartbroken because I needed to go back to Texas and I couldn't be with my girlfriend at the time, Megan. She lived in Michigan.
So, I thought about it for a minute or two and decided.

Yup, I'm moving to Michigan and transferring universities to continue this relationship with this girl I've known for a few weeks. I can get a job, it will be great. My parents didn't think so, but they didn't stop me. They didn't tell me I couldn't do it, or that I was crazy or stupid.

So, after ten months in Mount Pleasant, Michigan, Megan and I were boarding a flight to Norway to study abroad together in Prague, Czechia for five months. Of course, I hadn't given it much thought other than, *"Yes, I wanna go!"* Thankfully Megan actually had a head over her shoulders and looked into financial aid, programs, and whatnot.

Without knowing it, the flame that fed my desire to live abroad had been lit. I visited more than twenty countries, opened my mind, and realized that the world is simply a playground. Anybody brave enough to want to play in it, could!

After our time abroad, Megan and I broke up and I went back to Texas. Yes, happy to see my old friends and my mom. But in reality, deep inside, I was in agony reminiscing about my time abroad and decided to follow the voice telling me, *"You need to get the fuck out of here and keep exploring that playground you were just at! Go for it! Why not? What have you got to lose?"*

Poom! I'm in Europe with my best friend Alex right after

graduating from UTEP with the little money I had saved up.

Poom! Again, I get pickpocketed by a fourteen-year-old giving us directions for the metro on my first day abroad, literally within two hours of landing in France. I'm down 600 euros and have lost all my IDs and bank cards. *Yay me!*

"But, fuck it! Go with it and keep moving forward."

So, there I was. Finally where I had wanted to be! That freedom is incomparable, days stop having hours, mornings, and evenings. But rather you start counting in chunks or stages. For example, We've got thirty-six hours in Lyon, France during the 2016 Football UEFA Euro-Cup.

What should we do to make the most of it?

First, let's hit the town, get the feel of the city, see some landmarks and attractions, and try different foods. Then we'll stop at the pub to watch the semi-final game of Germany vs. France in the evening and see if we can make it till the A.M. to take some pictures of our favorite landmarks with the sunrise and before the crowd of tourists floods the streets.

Oh did I mention that I almost got into a hooligan street fight that night because of wearing my green Mexican football jersey?

At the time Germany's third kid was the same shade of green as Mexico and a big group of French fans thought I was German. There I was surrounded by ten aggressive French men ready to fight me! I put on the act of my life and acted as Mexican as I could to get out of the situation. *Boy, was that scary!*

I was however living in the moment. The countless magnificent, horrific, funny, sad, memorable, and dangerous experiences and both smart and stupid decisions Alex and I shared in Europe together made me start appreciating life by living in the moment and not by reminiscing about the past or dwelling on what the future would hold.

I went abroad because of my inability to make a life decision. I was escaping corporate life, the rat race, whatever that is. Life is full of twists and turns, and we often don't have much of a say regarding where we end up working, or what we end up doing to make a living and get by.

My life as a digital nomad came from the fact that I actually got on the plane, I actually met the locals, and struggled to get around every day because of language, culture, or other barriers. But the point is, my time abroad manifested into something real, with real opportunities, real friends, and anything else I could have wished for it to be.

How Did People React?

I guess I could say my family and friends expected it from me to go abroad and live differently, but I had never thought of it myself. I guess I never gave it much thought at all. As an only child, telling your parents your decision of, *"I'm leaving home and taking a chance"* is tough. Traditions, expectations, upbringings, and culture may come in the way of this easily. Luckily, my parents have been nothing but supportive of my desire to see what's out there.

I read once somewhere that travelers are the most selfish people. That stuck with me. I related to that a lot because as a traveler you live a lonelier life in some respects and choose to leave those dear to you behind.

We are always on the go, changing, "unstable" as some may view it. Boy, talk about how hard it is to get into a serious relationship when you are a nomad. But that topic is for another time.

Digital Nomads and expats who live abroad do share a superpower though. Our instinct of survival is sharp and we will do anything it takes to get it done.

Have you heard the saying in Spanish, entre la espada y la pared, meaning, between the sword and the wall? When you have no other choice but to act and get through it and survive no matter what.

That primal instinct we all have to survive no matter what.

"I don't know how I am going to make it to the embassy in Belgium the day after my passport got stolen in Ghent at a festival because someone took my bag from Alex's hands while he was taking a nap. But I am gonna get there and I am going to fix this!"

Thank god my passport expires in 2026 and I will never have to look at that picture again though. I walked fourteen kilometers that day with no sleep and no food in me. So when the embassy photographer told me to smile, you can probably imagine the layer of dirt and the stinky sweat and bitter rancid smell that engulfed my body that day. But, I got it done!

My High-Five Formula For Making Dreams Come True

This sharpened survival superpower is also practiced when we need to find a bathroom in the middle of a small village in Croatia and we need to overcome language barriers. Suddenly you put forward an Oscar-worthy charade performance to describe what you need because you are not thinking of being embarrassed or looking silly. You have an objective in mind and you will do anything in your power to get it done smoothly, efficiently, and quickly. No matter if you have to squat and make farting noises in front of strangers to get it done.

This power can then be mastered not only to overcome cultural differences or language barriers. But molded into hunger, readiness to take and seize any opportunity that comes your way, plan and take the best course of action to make it happen. You end up enjoying failure and mistakes because you know you can learn and grow from them. For my Ted talk in Hanoi, I was going to share my high-five formula for making dreams come true.

Put your hand up with all five fingers up.

It goes like this.

1. Dream

2. Do

3. Fail

4. Adapt

5. Repeat.

It's a lifelong learning experience and a game-based approach to life. The pleasure of learning through failure, noting the lessons, adapting, and trying again attitude.

That mentality I had been practicing is what also got me through my first three months in Vietnam as I discovered the English language market in Hanoi. I went all around this chaotic and colossal city doing class covers for students of all levels and ages, sometimes twenty kilometers away from my home while riding on a fifty-year-old rusty bicycle with a baby seat my friend Ivonna had lent me to get around my first three months while I saved to buy a motorcycle. I used to get to class with oily and black-stained hands because the chain of the bicycle would pop off a few times on my way to class, then I would ride back home in the evening. I didn't have a second to complain about my situation, I was in survival action mode! Without even thinking about it once, my educational career had started.

Many major events influenced me during my life. They've made me more mature, more wise and I like looking at the positive side of every outcome no matter how bad it may seem at the time.

The three lessons I learned while traveling and following my gut are that:

1. There will always be enough to keep moving forward. Put good out into the world and you will get good back. It's what we have always heard about karma, the universe has a very peculiar way of showing you this. But this positive manifestation is real.

2. You *can* do it! Whether you find yourself between a sword and a wall or you have set your mind to accomplish something you can do it. It may be messy, take longer than expected, and turn out differently than what you had thought. But you CAN do it!

3. You will be amazed to see the possibilities and the true limit of what can be possible once you are in motion and your journey has started. Every step of the way will answer your doubts and questions sustainably. You are building and working towards your goals and dreams, and while you do that, you will be amazed to realize that you will grow even further than what you had thought to be possible. Consistency, discipline, passion, and having fun in the process are necessary. If you do what you love, and you love what you do. Things will fall into place as long as you stay in motion.

No, I don't have everything figured out yet. But I do trust the process and I've seen the results of what consistency can lead to. There is somewhat of a curse when it comes to being a digital nomad, or a blessing as I see it myself. I am an ed-techpreneur, a founder, an academic director, a teacher trainer, a curriculum assessor, a student exchange coordinator, a marketing specialist, a content creator, a voice actor, a guide for outdoor field trips and excursions, a creative mind, and a start-up enthusiast. My plans for the near future are to continue developing my online projects under Link Online Learners while continuing to develop my network and my projects on the ground in Vietnam.

I'm not too focused on the destination, but rather, I enjoy every step of my journey and value the opportunity I have every day to do what I love. I wouldn't change my life or my messy hard to understand work for anything in the world. I believe I am influencing people, students, and dreamers in my own way, and I enjoy my day-to-day life.

I also plan on continuing to travel, forever and ever. When I die, I will be able to say that I have traveled to more countries than my age at that time. I'm thirty-one, as I am writing this in 2024, and I have traveled to thirty-two countries so far. I am not going to allow my age to catch up to the countries I visit.

Thank you for listening to my story. I hope that my optimism and positively charged energy can transcend the page and encourage you to dream and do. You are capable of anything you set your mind to, and you will find kindness along your path when you follow your passion and dreams. Live a life you are proud of. Live every day with no regrets, and enjoy every moment as it would be your last.

The most delicious drink in the world is not in some five-star restaurant or some VIP lounge somewhere. The most delicious drink in the world is the one you are drinking now. As you read this book.

AUTHOR HECTOR GRIMALDO

Hector Grimaldo is a Dreamer and a Doer. His friends and family call him Son Goku, as his personality matches with that of the friendly and optimistic character from Dragon Ball.

Hector is working to help dream, create, connect, and help scale innovative projects and opportunities that share a vision of a better future.

Hector wants to motivate, train, and guide students and schools to be part of this new era of Technology in education. Furthermore, he aims to serve in making valuable quality education available to all.

With networks like Link Online Learners, HundrED, Teach Millions, and LinkPower Hector is leading international education partnerships through creative collaborative thinking and project management training.

Connect with Hector:

https://linktr.ee/hectorgrimaldo

Phone: +522991578222 +84327574593

Email: hec.grimaldo@gmail.com

CHAPTER 9: COMFORTABLY UNCOMFORTABLE

By Vincent Reed

I started traveling while I was in my mother's womb. So I guess I'll start there. Just to give you a bit of context of who I am. She was pregnant with me on my first transatlantic flight to Ireland. The first of many.

Although I was born in small town Arkansas, I also was born into a traveling, expat abroad-living family. Family on both sides of the pond in Europe and North America that later spread into the Middle East and Asia.

My mom is Irish and my dad is American. They met while both teaching English in Madrid in the 1980s. One escaping the troubles of Belfast and the other getting out from under his father's shadow.

Suppose we're all escaping or chasing something right?

My dad eventually brought my mom back to America to get married and start a family. All my aunts and uncles on both sides left home in their twenties to pursue something different and a life elsewhere. My grandfather, that shadow I mentioned, was a foreign correspondent for *The New York Times* during the 1960s and 70s so you can imagine the treasure trove of stories I got from him over the years.

Long story short, this sort of escapism route comes naturally to me so to speak. Certainly runs in the family. Studying abroad, stuffing my life into a bag, airplane food, smelly train stations, asking for directions, changing money, wandering in foreign cities - this has been my life essentially all my life. And I fucking love it.

While stability and security are great and can't be overlooked - finding your way in the world through becoming an expat, relocating yourself, and adapting to new surroundings is the best teacher and classroom out there in my opinion. And at a far more reasonable price in the long term than Western education and modern comforts that will cripple us both financially and mentally. But I'll get to that later.

So anyway, back to my story. I was born and raised in the good ole US of A but spent every other summer in Ireland growing up. The funny accents and afternoon tea and biscuits grew on me.

My mother was a Spanish language teacher so as teenagers my brother and I went on the occasional Europe trip with her and her junior high students that included pit stops in Rome, Paris, Athens, Heidelberg, Madrid, and Venice. These summer trips opened my eyes to life on the road as a tourist.

I distinctly remember a gondola ride in Venice and staring down into the mysterious canals and then up at church steeples dotting the Venetian skyline and thinking, *"Wow, I've never seen anything like this in Arkansas, this is pretty cool."*

I also recall wandering around the Roman Colosseum with my high school buddies and thinking to ourselves, *"We're not in Little Rock anymore."*

My first solo trip was when I was fifteen and went to Guatemala on a high school spring break trip to study Spanish and live with a local host family. Being my first third-world country experience and without my parents for the first time, I was culturally but pleasantly shocked in more ways than one. I'll get to that later too.

I then studied abroad in Barcelona my third year of university which really broadened my horizons to actual day-to-day life in a foreign city and how it worked. I lived with a host mother/local senora who became like a second mother while Spain became like a second home.

Funny when people ask me what major I studied in university and I tell them international relations, the only reason I chose that field was because it was required to study abroad in order to graduate. I was an easy sell on that one.

After graduation, it was only right to follow in my parent's footsteps and teach English overseas. Besides, I didn't really know what the hell I wanted to do and lacked any direction other than where my local airport was, and that I preferred a window seat.

It was then that my Dad challenged me to go somewhere completely different. I was thinking of going back to Spain to find work because of my familiarity with the language and culture and having loved my time in Barcelona just two years prior.

He mentioned China. And I thought, *"China? Why on earth would I go there?"* I don't know anyone there, don't speak the language, it's a long way from anywhere and I know hardly anything about the country.

At twenty-two years old, little did I know those reasons above are exactly why you should say yes to a place like China. Fast forward a bit and I get my graduation credits sorted, deliver sandwiches during the summer for some extra cash, and finally, I'm in Hangzhou, China, a massive bustling city about an hour and a half from Shanghai on the east coast that I'd never heard of.

Almost immediately upon arrival, I met a community of

Canadian expats who had been living there for a few years and working as TEFL teachers. I very quickly felt this feeling of camaraderie among these guys. Whether it was learning to play hockey, watching the Super Bowl at an ungodly hour in the morning, street meat and beers after work, riding electric bikes around the city, exploring other Chinese sites or just getting help with the weekly lesson planning, I felt a feeling of belonging but also a reassuring feeling of adventure with my life, knowing that I was doing something not many people would even dream of doing with their lives: living in a Far East country, not knowing the language, figuring out how to teach English, finding a job and a random group of friends to show me the ropes, eating weird food, learning how to bargain at local markets, just navigating life as a foreigner in a foreign land.

I absolutely loved my time there and still keep in touch with a couple of the Canadian guys but very efficiently drank, partied, and weekend-traveled all my money away and ultimately had to go back to the U.S. to live with my mom a year later. Rude awakening but a good wake-up call nonetheless. One that we all have to experience at some point in time.

Originally after coming home from China in 2013, I told myself I'd stay only a few months, live at home, collect a few paychecks, and then get back to Hangzhou with my newfound community of like-minded expats and travelers. However, that plan turned out to be a bit ambitious and I soon realized that it would take at least a couple of years to not only save up a sufficient amount to be able to comfortably leave but also be stable abroad while reestablishing myself.

After living at home for a couple of years, working multiple jobs as a valet and waiter and saving as much as I could, in late 2016 I bought a one-way ticket to Hanoi, Vietnam to rekindle my expat dream and continue in my family's footsteps of working and living in foreign lands far from home.

So, why Vietnam, you ask?

Mainly I'd heard a lot of good things from trusted travelers and family members who had been. Cost of living, cuisine, opportunity, good airport, gorgeous scenery, and the women among other things. Its proximity to China and possibly popping up to see my old buddies helped in making my decision too. So I did some research and said fuck it.

I also contacted the Asia bug. If any of you have been to Asia, maybe you know what I'm referring to. There's just something about life in Asia, specifically Southeast Asia, that is just magnetizing and hard to let go of. It probably has something to do with what I mentioned above but it's also something abstract that you can't quite see or put your finger on. While it's not in Southeast Asia, China gave me a sneak peek and a teaser into what life could really be like in this part of the world.

Oh and remember those reasons I told myself why I shouldn't consider a move to China after graduating?

Well, those were all reasons why I wound up saying yes to Vietnam: I didn't know anyone, didn't know Vietnamese and sadly, apart from the Vietnam War, I knew nothing about the country.

So Vincent, why are you telling us all this?

Well first to just give you a brief summary and snapshot into my life and where I come from. But secondly and more importantly, I believe whoever you are reading this, you and I can relate or connect somehow through this little chapter of mine.

Maybe it's the expat life you're interested in, maybe you're enticed by Vietnam, maybe you're living at home like I was before moving abroad, maybe you're from small town U.S.A, maybe you have divorced or well-traveled parents like me, maybe you're lacking direction like I once was, maybe you've never left your hometown like most of my friends, or maybe you want to return to your home country, a feeling that most expats have struggled with at one point or another.

Whatever your situation or circumstance is, I thank you for reading this far and encourage you to keep reading to potentially find what you're looking for.

The first thing I want to bring up is the comfort zone. I think it was Marcus Aurelius or maybe it was just a *LinkedIn* quote that said something along the lines of, *"Being comfortable is one of the most dangerous addictions to man,"* and, *"Life begins at the end of your comfort zone."*

There's a comfort zone when it comes to life, dating, your hometown, your job, what we eat, and so much more. A very enticing yet dangerous comfort zone. Of course, we all want to be comfortable. And there's nothing wrong with that. Comfort is nice, let's be honest. It's cozy and warm and has familiar faces and routines. What I want to address is that if a life abroad appeals to you, or if you're struggling while living abroad, or even struggling to get out of bed and go to work- then maybe the comfort zone trap should be taken into consideration.

Oh, and this isn't meant to be a self-help, look-at-me, listen-to-me, cause-I-made-it, and-live-the-dream type of chapter. That was one reason why I gave you some backstory on me. I haven't got it all figured out, I'm thirty-three and living in a basic studio apartment in Hanoi, Vietnam, teaching English and juggling a few side hustles that keep me going and content. I just love talking about this because I have seen how it has played a big role in my life the last few years in where I was and where I am now. I think getting out of your comfort zone is absolutely essential in the life of a nomad or expat who's living a bit of a different life than most.

Let's take a look at that first trip I went on without my parents. My first third-world country trip to Guatemala. I'm not sure I fully realized or appreciated it at the time, but that was a massive, *"F you!"* to the comfort zone type of trip at an early age. Traveling at fourteen without my loved ones, to a country with its fair share of violence and crime, immersing myself in a language, culture, and customs I knew next to nothing about. Free tableside chips and salsa and saying a playful, *"Hola!"* to the waitress at my local Mexican restaurant in Arkansas didn't really prepare me for what I experienced in Guatemala.

One of my first memories was arriving in Guatemala City and taking a coach bus to the nearby town where we were staying. I remember looking out the window and being amazed at just the amount of activity taking place on the street. The filth, the buying and selling, the pulsating music blasting, the smelly, shuffling livestock, and the constant yelling in a language that didn't sound like the Spanish I knew.

I had never seen so much happening on the street. So much stimulation. Remember, I was fourteen at the time. Granted, I have been to Europe multiple times, but Western Europe and Central America are two very different animals. And speaking of animals, don't get me started on the food. Cuisine is something I always seek out when traveling to new places and I believe trying local dishes is something absolutely essential when getting comfortably uncomfortable in unfamiliar surroundings whether you're touring or planning to settle somewhere.

I remember wandering out of class one day and wanting a quick bite and seeing a lady with a stall selling what looked like a taco salad and it smelled heavenly. I pointed or said something in my high school-level Spanish and she proceeded to pile a load of things on a crispy tortilla and hand it to me. It was probably less than a dollar and one of the most delicious things I'd ever tasted. Street food culture is something I'm very familiar with now living in Vietnam but at the time it was a concept I'd never been exposed to in Europe and certainly not in the United States.

I think it also helped pave the way and prepare and shape me for what was to come in terms of my future travels and endeavors. I think we can agree that after you do something uncomfortable or scary once, it becomes a little easier the second and third time and every other time going forward. Whether it's scuba diving, the first day of school, that first date or language lesson, your first solo trip, and so on.

Hell, even me writing this little chapter is uncomfortable and, in fact, me getting out of my comfort zone. Easier said than done obviously.

Had I not gone to Guatemala, who knows, maybe I never would've branched out and traveled to China and in turn probably wouldn't be living in Vietnam as we speak for as long as I have.

The disturbing and stimulating sights and smells, the confusing streets and alleys, not understanding the menu, getting looked at with caution and curiosity, awkwardly asking for directions- these are little life lessons we learn when abroad and on our own that massively improve our critical thinking, self-confidence, self-esteem and decision making that we most likely don't even recognize at the time of dealing with them.

When people ask me questions like why I live in Vietnam, how I've managed so long over here, if I'm homesick, or why I travel so much, they are speaking from a place of comfort. A place of regularity and routine and knowing. And that's totally ok.

You simply don't know what you don't know.

I think my answer to all those questions above could be as simple as, well, I got out of my comfort zone and went and did it and just figured it out along the way. Explored the streets, got lost, was misunderstood or laughed at, tried the food, spit it out, started dating, went for that strange interview, said yes when I might normally say no, or whatever the case may be.

You learn by doing. That uncomfortable feeling brings out the necessity but also the adventure in us. You learn when you're lost, you learn when you fail, you learn when you get pickpocketed, you learn when you're alone, and you learn when you're hungry.

Does that make sense?

I truly believe that when one makes the conscious decision to venture out of that comfortable place and dive into a new life abroad or even just tackle a new, possibly long-lost idea, life becomes pretty sweet.

It could be that business plan you've had bottled up for years, moving out of your mom's spare room, asking that cute girl or guy out, saying yes to hang-gliding, going on that safari with your partner or just trying that new Ethiopian restaurant in your neighborhood.

In most cases, you'd be surprised at what you can handle and how much you actually like doing new shit. And how a whole new perspective and thrill with life is located on that other side of fear that's holding you back.

I do have to warn you though - doing these fun, new exciting things can be addicting and hard to stop. I've heard the same from people with getting tattoos or adrenaline seekers, you're always thinking about and looking for the next one.

That leads me to my last point. Last but not certainly not least: life is all about balance and awareness. I think there are some people in my hometown who assume I just travel ALL the time since I'm over on the other side of the world. Or they think I'm living a jam-packed, fun-filled, adventure everyday type of lifestyle. While mine or other social media accounts might portray that from time to time, it's simply not the case.

Do I travel more than most Americans? Yes.

Do I have my fair share of interesting adventures and stories to tell my future grandkids? Yes.

Do I live in an Asian capital metropolis-type city with no shortage of things to do? Yes.

However, I also have my little daily routine that some might find boring, my local coffee shop and grocery like anyone else, and my route to work which can be hectic and exhausting. I do menial, energy-draining things like anyone else on this planet. I suppose it's all relative and occasionally we all get a case of comparisonitis. Looking at other people's lives and wishing it was our own. Comparing our front yard to our neighbors. Seeing that someone got a new iPhone or gadget so they feel obligated to upgrade theirs. Examining others' travel photos and wishing we were there. That has to stop.

While it can serve as good motivation to book your next trip or kick a bad habit, looking at others' lives whether it is family members, good friends, or just friends of friends, and letting their lives and situations take away from your own is not the way to live a true life in the present. One thing travel will undoubtedly give you is a sense of gratitude and how well you have it, especially if you're from the Western world. How much we can afford, how much we physically own and have access to in our respective countries and hometowns.

With all this being said, life is meant to be lived. Lived by each of us individually.

AUTHOR
VINCENT REED

Vincent is a thirty-three-year-old Irish-American expat who has been living in Hanoi, Vietnam since 2017.

His day job is teaching English to anyone who wants to hear his sweet Southern accent, but he also dabbles in trading, affiliate and social media marketing, crypto, and a few other side hustles to keep him mobile, remote, and happy.

In his free time, Vincent loves spy novels, sampling new local cuisine, walks in the park or up a mountain, an iced coffee with a view, and of course adding new stamps to his passport collection.

If you'd like to follow along his journey or privately reach out to him with any questions, he's most active on Instagram as @vincereedonline.

ABOUT NOMAD PUBLISHING

We offer writing support and publishing services to aspiring travel authors.

See our other titles:

Nomads: Adventurous Businesswomen That are Changing the World While Traveling

Born to Travel: Wanderlust Families that Collect Passport Stamps Instead of Toys

BOOK THE FLIGHT ALREADY!: Travelers Share Their Life-Changing Stories from Off-the-Beaten-Track Bucket List Trips

Worldschoolers: Innovative Parents Turning Countries into Classrooms

Digital Nomad Moms: Women who Carved Out Successful Remote Careers to Travel the World with their Children

Freedom: Travel-Loving Single Moms who Found Flexibility

and Financial Independence through Remote Work

Outside the Box: Traveling Families that Work, Educate, and Live on Their Own Terms

For more information on publishing services, contact Sara Tyler directly by text message (+52 56 5050 2513) or WhatsApp: https://wa.me/message/CJRWPOME3VRJD1